this journey
a path to simple enlightenment

suni moon

Copyright © 2024 Suni Moon, Journey Studios LLC

All rights reserved. You may not sell or reproduce any part of this book without written consent from the copyright owner.

There is information in this book regarding health and wellness. This book is intended to be educational and not for diagnosis or treatment of any health disorder. This information cannot replace consultation with your health care professional. The information is intended as an adjunct to a rational and responsible health care program prescribed by a professional healthcare practitioner. The author and publisher are not in any way liable for misuse of this information.

First paperback edition December 2024

Book design by Journey Studios
Cover photography and original painting by Suni Moon
Illustrations by Suni Moon

ISBN-979-8-9921110-0-2

Library of Congress Control Number: 2024925433

JourneyStudios.com
SuniMoon.net

Table of Contents

Introduction 1

Part one- What went wrong, how to right it ...5

1. Simple enlightenment 7
2. This changed world 13
3. The broken world we came from 17
4. The new world is here 23
5. Global awakening, emotional maturity 29
6. New world- new you 35
7. Body + spirit = you 39
8. Living in fear 43
9. A higher path, how to empower others 47
10. Now is the time and you are ready 51

Part two- Taking action 55

11. Where it started for me 57
12. Labels we wear 61
13. Your bright sparks from childhood 67
14. Learn to be the observer of your mind 71
15. Aspects of consciousness 77
16. Connecting to the body 81
17. What is light 85
18. Your body's energy system 91

19. Using energy in healing 97
20. Intention and visualization 103
21. Your inner wisdom is infallible 109
22. Teach from within 113
23. Breathe- to listen and empower 117
24. Your voice and its power 123
25. True love is found through self love 129
26. The body is a natural healer 133
27. Self-care is world care 139
28. Meditation your way 143
29. Going deeper 149
30. Channeling your highest self 153
31. Power of nature and forest bathing 159
32. Creating ritual and ceremony 163
33. Sound- a healing energy 171
34. Stones- healers in the earth 177
35. Connection and community 183
36. In closing 185

More about the author 187

References 188

Index

this journey

This book is dedicated to all the seekers. Some of us found our clans, others of us never quite fit. Your constant wondering/wandering can slow down as now is our time. We all can fit in now. The world needs us and our unique purposes. Find your enlightenment right inside your heart then join me. Let's go help build this new world.

The cover painting is titled Oneness and was created by Suni Moon. This image of many different energies/ colors/ beings has been with Suni for decades. The design has popped up again and again, in many painted iterations that have found homes in many hearts. It is a time in our world where many of us are experiencing the power of finding community to be and build more. The many can act as one in peace, love and compassion. Reproductions or commissions of similar works can be explored at JourneyStudios.com.

This icon reminds you that all the meditation and guided practices are available online.
Visit SuniMoon.net/readers

Introduction

I just wanted to be normal, just wanted to fit in. I needed to understand the rules of life. I felt like you all had a rulebook, but I didn't. It turns out, most of us are missing the rule book. We have bits and pieces here and there- a paper trail or breadcrumbs along the path. That is certainly how it worked for me. I intend this book to help you see your breadcrumbs more clearly. Hopefully, this story will help you appreciate the little gifts you've received along the way. May this be a reminder to you to revisit the lessons that were bright and warm as well as the times that were hard and cold- considering all of those together. They are the story of you, as this book is a story of me. Join me on my winding journey as I try to explain how I figured out that, indeed, I do have an inner rule book, an inner guidance system, and I know you do too.

I am a teacher and a healer. I work with individuals and small groups, leading a class today, and two people coming for one-on-one appointments tomorrow. In each of those encounters, I intuitively share insights or healing sound and energy. When we all part ways, I wonder if I helped. I hope I helped. At the end of the day, I think, "What is it I do?" What am I here to teach? Better yet, what do I believe? I have an amazing lifetime of experiences and adventures that have made me who I am. But is there a class I could teach that might pull the experiences together to help others? Is there a breathwork practice or a beautiful sound meditation that can transmit the magic I feel in my heart? Recently, I have looked back at all the adventures and began seeing how the pieces fit together. How this or that experience does make sense looking back. Maybe there IS purpose to all that happened. I can see how the thing that happened 40 years ago makes more sense standing beside the thing that happened 20 years ago. Purposes are even clearer when I put those lessons beside the thing that happened 2 years ago or the new bit I learned yesterday. I began to sense how all the pieces together have made me feel whole and complete.

this *journey*

I have the sort of brain that can't make sense of a bunch of ideas floating around in my head. I need to write things down to sort them out. So to share whatever I've learned from life, I needed to write. I started small... writing ideas that seemed important to share on pieces of paper. I put the papers in a basket on the corner of my desk. Whenever I had a brain fart about an idea or memory that played into the grand idea (whatever that was), I wrote it on a scrap of paper and put it in the basket. Some days, adding five or six- some days none. This went on for months. My jumbled mess of things that I had learned along the way- ideas and experiences that helped me so much on my path from lost to found, from broken to healed, all piled up in that basket. Until that point, I really couldn't tell people about the bigger picture of my teaching. I could lead a workshop on this or that subject. I could do a healing session to help another, but what was the goal of it all? I couldn't even tell those closest to me what all of those little bits of wisdom meant. So I dumped that basket out on the kitchen floor and started sorting it into categories. Categories became chapters and chapters became this book.

I'm not the most eloquent writer, however I've proven to be quite good at living a full life. I'm fantastic at finding answers to my questions and as it turns out, I'm quite experienced in listening to my higher self. So here's the story of how I figured out a path that for me, led to embracing my beautiful little purpose. My life shines with more peace and meaning than I ever imagined back when I started reading other people's rule books. This book is my way of sharing my winding path with you. And to encourage you that yours is also right beneath your feet, right now, today.

Simple enlightenment is attainment of a clarity, energy, compassion, peace, fairness, kindness and more. Simple enlightenment is no less amazing and powerful than the awakening, samadhi or nirvana of other traditions. I believe it happens when each of us can embrace and employ our physical, mental, emotional, and spiritual selves in union, in our own unique lives. You have simple enlightenment. You were born with it.

This simple approach works for me. I think it opens the door to higher self for many people, especially people who don't see themselves as mystics or spiritual explorers. I resonate with folks who are finding their own path, their own true expression. All paths to the higher self are valid. If you're seeking some wise guru who will tell you exactly what to do, you won't find that here. I don't offer you deep explanations or strict practices. There are many other books and traditions that work that way. Are you looking for some basic direction then prefer to go blaze your own trail? Then this simple path might fit you just right.

I wish all of us can learn to sit still with ourselves. That's when we get to know our real identity, explore our true purposes, peel off the labels that society smacked on us, and realize there is nothing wrong with us. We begin to see ourselves and our purposes more clearly. We perceive our path right here and now, not floating nebulously in the future. Can we embrace the idea that there is an invisible part of ourselves that will last well beyond the time our body falls apart? When we connect that invisible aspect, that spirit or energy, with the more familiar physical self, then all the tumblers of the lock can click in. You have enlightenment that you can access whenever you need to. While you still live in our transforming world, you can call back your own sense of calm and peace whenever needed. You always have access to a higher, wiser, calmer self to empower you to build your best life and help your family, community, world do the same. I can teach you this. I can tell you all about the stuff that I explored that works. Study what I'm sharing, and a conduct few research journeys of your own and find your simple enlightenment too.

4   this *journey*

 This icon reminds you that all the meditation and sound practices are available online.
Visit SuniMoon.net/readers

part one

What went wrong and how to right it

Your life is your journey. The goal is to enjoy, embrace… really embody the being you are meant to be, savoring your steps along the path of life. The goal is to be you, with grace and power, with health and happiness. Wherever you are on your path, or if you're seeking your path, this book is for you. We are all right where we're supposed to be. Experiencing your power and wisdom doesn't come "some day." It should come today, every day. Now is your time and you are ready.

this journey

Simple enlightenment

I was seeking more in my life. Where is my nirvana, the Samadhi, the host of heavenly angels singing? But life never brought me those big mystical awakenings. I was drawn to study and practice the metaphysical, but never resonated with finding spirit guides that talk to me. I felt fake if I would call in this archangel or that. I explored many traditions and religions. I always found the most peaceful direction within myself, naturally and alone. I found a knowing inside that I could trust. Life went on and eventually I discovered the path I'm on is working really well for me. I have connected to my higher self and that brings me a power and peace beyond anything I hoped for.

When I unite my physical, visible, logical self with my aspects of spirit, the invisible, the magical- all the pieces click together for me. I found something I can rely on. There is a great power within me. I didn't have to call out into the darkness and hope something heard me and came to help. My higher wisdom is always here inside me. My gut was always onboard to give me direction and help make choices. I realized that this intuition or direction is a very simple, practical, accessible and understandable form of light/spirit/source. This internal voice is something I could actually explain to people. I knew that I wasn't the only one wired this way. So here we are.

physical and *spiritual*

visible & *invisible*

practical + *magical*

this journey

I know my use of the term "simple enlightenment" will raise a few eyebrows. Many of us associate enlightenment with a difficult-to-reach state of spiritual knowledge that some study a lifetime for and few feel they achieve. The term enlightenment has a perceived religious connection, as does the word spiritual. The association with religion makes some folks resist the idea of enlightenment, as they don't see themselves as religious. I am sure that many of us might wish for enlightenment, but we feel challenged to actually define it. So I have concluded that my title might crank some people off, but the truth is most of us see enlightenment as something outside of our reach or potential. So I have chosen to remain unconcerned about my use of a word that most people have written off, anyway? (grin) Rather than judge me, allow me to bring a fresh focus to enlightenment and explore why you have found yourself drawn to this open-to-question term.

To clarify, let's define the word enlightenment.[1]

> *enlightenment*
> 1. the action of enlightening or the state of being enlightened. Similar words: understanding, insight, education, learning, knowledge, awareness, information, wisdom, instruction, teaching, illumination, light, edification, awakening, refinement, cultivation, civilization, sophistication, advancement, development, broad-mindedness, an aha moment. The action or state of attaining or having attained spiritual knowledge or insight,
> 2. a European intellectual movement of the late 17th and 18th centuries emphasizing reason and individualism rather than tradition.
> 3. Suni's definition- A state of deep knowledge which allows us to live in purpose, peace, serenity, bliss as we choose to. We engage this natural state when we live as physical and spiritual beings, using the powers of both aspects together.

Notice the similar words in the dictionary definition. Most of those words are things that we all seek. Funny how the word enlightenment feels out-of-reach to many of us. In this book, I'm bringing you a message that enlightenment IS for all of us. I believe you were born enlightened. I hope to help you find your way back to that truth.

We are living in changed times. Note I didn't use the word changing, but changed. There is a new energy here on the planet. I and many others see this new energy as supporting global awakening. That's a big statement to wrap your brain around. As the book progresses, I'll touch on many aspects of this changed world that might facilitate your seeing the changes more clearly. For now, imagine that our changed world has rewritten the rules, the roles and the ideals. In this new world, simple enlightenment means seeing oneself as not just physical, mental, emotional, but also connecting to and using the wisdom of the spiritual/energetic self. I am referring to spirit as an energy, your life force energy. Spirit/energy is the part of you that hangs around after your body has worn out. This is the invisible you, the ah-ha moment you, the "where did that great idea come from" you.

The energy of spirit, the invisible, is in us all. You might consider yourself an atheist. That title doesn't remove you from the world of energy/spirit. Science has hit a wall in research where, sometimes, they just can't explain things. Einstein used a phrase, "spooky action at a distance" to describe the phenomenon of entanglement. He couldn't explain it based on knowledge of the time; therefore, he labeled all of quantum mechanics as wrong. But, in the 1980s, entanglement was validated as an entirely new kind of phenomenon. We have entered a world where many things cannot always be explained as true or false, black or white. It is a time to open to energies in life that we don't totally understand. I'm calling one of those energies your spirit or consciousness. Consciousness is becoming part of science. Consciousness studies explore this undefinable term combining perspectives from philosophy, science, and spirituality. I suggest we all remain open to the idea that there is some spark of life or consciousness, a part of the human body that doesn't show up on the anatomy chart.

It is key as we try to navigate this changed world, to find a connection to our energetic self, our higher wisdom, our spiritual self, our magic. This book's purpose is to provide information, simple exercises and practices that you can explore to strengthen your connection to the higher self, to the spirit. I didn't make up these practices, nor am I channeling them from some higher place. These are ideas/practices that I've gleaned from a lifetime of study- seeking the keys to happiness, success, and purpose in my own life. I have found within some cultures, at the root of some religions, in modern research and higher thinking- that there are common threads and basic tenets. Understanding these common threads or keys has opened many doors for me to my higher self and deeper purpose in life.

this *journey*

Our spirit or energetic self is not greater or finer than our physical self, with which we are more familiar. Our spirit self has skills that our visible body does not. Likewise, the spirit/energetic self becomes empowered by living in a body and can take actions that spirit alone cannot. I am calling on you to realize and strengthen your connection with that spiritual/energetic side of you. Embrace the spiritual, not to the exception of the physical. The key is to understand that those two aspects of you together is where your enlightenment lies. The spirit can't accomplish the same things alone as it can when housed in a physical body. Most of us have experienced life as physical beings without honoring or using our energetic aspects. Now is the time to bring spirit into your everyday life. Our spirit self isn't just for praying or meditating. I like to imagine we can get comfortable in our body/spirit package when asking directions or listening to a friend in need.

I don't ask anyone to follow me or to believe what I believe. I wish to help you build a "toolkit" to deepen your connection to your higher self. I hope to show paths allow you to make and define this connection to the higher you <u>in your own way</u>. It is only by making this adventure very personal that you connect with your unique strengths and purpose. There is no one path to becoming your best you. Open and allow, receive and release as you see fit.

You will not find any in-depth dissertations here on individual subjects. I open doors for you that you may not have considered wandering through before. If the concept of meditation your way, or the healing power of your own energy resonates with you, then I trust you will take the small flame that gets ignited here and go learn more. I'm just your guide as we tour the concept of individual enlightenment being your birthright. I trust you will grab onto any topic that lifts you and go dive deeper into the exploration of you.

As you explore your true purpose, also consider that enlightenment isn't just an individual experience. We are living in a time when it has become crucial that we find enlightenment to open us to our role in the community, the whole. As we open our eyes to our true power, may we realize as mature adults, our role is to serve our tribe, our community, our world through love and compassion.

To connect your physical with your spiritual is my challenge to you. This is the simple enlightenment I speak of. Enlightenment means realizing all you are. That doesn't require decades of study with a guru, isolating in a cave on a mountainside. It only requires you to learn to look within you.

> *"The moment of awakening may be marked by an outburst of laughter, but this is not the laughter of someone who has won the lottery or some kind of victory. It is the laughter of one who, after searching for something for a long time, suddenly finds it in the pocket of his coat."*
> *- Thich Nhat Hanh, Zen Keys: A Guide to Zen Practice*[2]

Simple enlightenment is for you

The concept of simple enlightenment is to free you. You aren't striving for some unattainable perfection. You have it all right now. You are a lovely blend of physical and spiritual, human and light, perfect and imperfect. You are all this right now, today and every day. Even the days when you wake up on the wrong side of the bed to find the dog peed in your shoe and you're out of coffee. Every day, breathe deep, you are the light.

Simple enlightenment is for the world

This simple enlightenment is not just for you, or for me. It is not individual enlightenment so you can sleep better at night and quit getting lost in your fears. It's so much greater than that. It is enlightenment for all. We need to connect our human and spirit for all people, for our world, so that we can work together to help more people find their higher wisdom. The new world, the new energy, is calling us to become true adults, taking our place in the community. I wrote this book to help me, to help you, and to help us all get to the next level.

this journey

This changed world

How are you feeling in this changed world? Are you longing for the good old days? Feeling fearful of what might be coming? Are you busy seeking to place blame, or to find the one who can fix all this?

Any of these feelings are understandable. We were raised in the old world ruled by the energies of fear and greed. That world is fading away. There is a new world here, but we've become so ingrained in the "old ways" that it feels impossible that they can ever change. But the world has and will continue to change. The challenge for each of us is to change ourselves so we can see and assist the new world. We change, our lives and actions change, and those shifts allow others to see the changed world too.

Yes, I understand that if you're still stuck in the belief that the world can never change, I sound deluded. I ask you to imagine, just for a few more chapters, that what I'm saying might be true. As an experiment, just play with the idea. I'll explain more as we move along. But I need you to open your heart and mind a bit. Take a long, deep breath and as you exhale, let a tiny bit of resistance go. You picked up this book seeking new ideas. So let's carry on and explore new ideas.

The new world is here. Energies have risen which empower you to do things you never could before. You are the one to help this world fulfill its potential. Your mission is to fulfill your true purpose and use your innate talents to support the planet by engaging with all around you in love and compassion. This is a tall order… in the old world, yes.

There are many paths to being your best self, finding your higher wisdom. My teaching often resonates with a seeker who may not see themselves as spiritual or woo-woo. Are you looking for ideas that feel comfortable and seem attainable? Things have changed and our paths to being our highest, best self are open as they never have been before.

this journey

Where we once knew the world as real only in the physical perspective, now we must learn to honor the spiritual or energetic aspect as well. In the old world, the visible was all that was "real" and now we must choose to embrace the invisible. While some still insist they will only believe the practical/logical explanations, we now have been endowed with the magical.

You are physical and spiritual.
You are visible and invisible.
You are practical/logical and magical.

When you embrace all aspects of yourself, there is an empowerment that occurs. You realize that there is more to you than meets the eye. There is more to life than who has the most money or the fanciest toys. We realize that we exist outside of our own skin. We begin to see value in all other people, not just the rich and famous. All of us can make time to find the wonder in nature, in a starry night sky. We come to cherish the feeling of a deep breath at an anxious moment. Seeing these dual aspects of life enables us to be more, see more, know more than we ever could before. Being all we can be opens us to embrace our own simple enlightenment.

I have found simple enlightenment and I want to share the basic practice with anyone who is seeking more. This isn't a religious experience. It doesn't even ask you to do things my way. I do not believe there is one path for all in this new world. I'll share simple tools gleaned from a lifetime of studying many traditions. The goal is simply to become a whole, mature human, ready to take a place in helping/serving the world. This wholeness or maturity comes from exploring basic skills of listening to yourself, grounding to something greater (earth, sky, spirit, ancestors, you, nature), then becoming your best you.

Sound too simple? Yeah, it's simple and no one will complicate it, <u>but you</u>. How do I know these practices will work? I've watched life in many cultures and religions, studied history and science to see that the answers, our wisdom and wonder <u>are all within</u>. I have also lived this path. I sought knowledge to fix my broken self. That has taken a long time and I'm still working on it.

I don't bring you new information. I teach you to forget a lot of old lies. I open doors so you might remember the real you. I suggest that all your life experiences (the lovely and the horrible) brought lessons and wisdom. I teach ways you can release the pain, the "hangover" of trauma, while retaining the power and wisdom that you carried away from those experiences by surviving and thriving. You can release karmic residue/life trauma and embrace your power, listen to wisdom within, stand and shine. You can become the real you. The whole complete unencumbered you is here for a purpose and you are ready now to serve that role. You are ready and now is your time.

Come with me as I share what I've learned to help you find your hope, excitement, and a new level of awakening in this new world. I hope to touch on many topics knowing that the ones that truly resonate with you will move you to find deeper resources on your own. Simple enlightenment is here. It's not down some winding road. It exists within you. You were born with this wondrous truth.

This first part of the book explains my concept, my understanding of what simple enlightenment is and how we connect with this beautiful power. Simple enlightenment is built into every being. But our old world did not help us learn to make the connection. We have forgotten how amazing we are and how to find our way back to our purpose, our power, and our simple enlightenment.

Part two of the book will introduce practices common on a spiritual path. This is a sort of guidebook to the land of the mystical. I'm covering the basics here so someone who maybe hasn't dabbled in the metaphysical (the beyond the physical) realm might enjoy these "Cliff Notes." I offer different topics to help you change your habits, releasing old limiting beliefs, and being open to new ideas.

I'm not recommending a deep dive into the land of woo-woo, calling in all archangels (unless, of course, archangels are your jam). I've chosen to share with you some basic concepts- light, energy, healing sound, breathing, meditation; all things that are part of life. These life tools are really helpful, elevating and energizing. I am not denying that finding a spirit guide or calling in the angels can be a lovely way to go for some. But those aspects of spiritual/energetic growth just never resonated with me. I hope here in this book you can find different ways to elevate, different tools to explore. Once you find your comfortable tools, then there are many books that will teach you much more.

this journey

I am an intuitive. I sense things. I have an inner knowing. I have some psychic abilities, but I can't contact your dear departed aunt Edna, and ask her where she hid the family jewels. I feel like I live on the edges of the land of woo. I know that magic exists. I feel strongly that its power exists in me, even if my approach lacks some bells and whistles of others. I believe in the mystical, but it seems to work best for me when I find it within. I've never felt that it was important for me to call in legions of angels or my spirit guides because I tend to turn within and get quiet. There I find my guidance, my wisdom, my fresh ideas.

This is my style of mysticism. And through a lifetime of learning how to accept this and grow into the experiences better, I was given the title and the concept for this book on simple enlightenment. It fits my MO. I didn't go off find a guru and isolate myself in the mountainside for 20 years. None of us have time for that sort of thing right now, as the world has changed into something brand new. I have touched enlightenment and I can touch it again when I need to. You can too, because you were born enlightened. The world tried to educate it and label it out of you. I hope to help you peel off the labels, to help you learn how to calm yourself, honor yourself and see yourself for the wonder you are and always have been. You truly are a beautiful being with purpose and you have a hotline to all the wisdom that ever was. Welcome to simple enlightenment. Come on a journey with me.

The broken world we came from

Our old world was broken. I don't intend to convey fear or hopelessness with that statement. Our world is/was unfair, unkind, filled with fear, unsustainable, uncaring, and not equitable. The old world valued money, power, greed, celebrity, growth and profits. Most importantly, our old world does not value or understand the critical importance of love and compassion.

The broken aspects of the world aren't all "out there," but also within each of us. Many of us carry brokenness inside- a sadness, a sense of being resigned to a day-to-day grind. Honoring only the physical aspects of ourselves and our world is a part of the brokenness. We believed in the magical aspects of life as children, but let go of those "fanciful things" when we grew up. Truth is, children believe in the physical and the magical and I hope to help you open to that perspective once again.

The old world called us to grow up, get a job, make good money, find "the one," buy a home and make little people to grow up and do more of the same. Money, acquisitions, conformity are all measures of our success. This mentality has created a world that sees having money as a measure of our value and power. That perspective causes greed to grow. More success is more stuff or money. All this in the physical realm, all outside of us.

Since the agricultural revolution, we have locked up housing and food. That terminology comes from Daniel Quinn's books[3], the Ishmael series. If you don't have enough money, you get no food, you have no home. We have many people in the US, living with no shelter, no steady source of healthy nutrition because our society has failed them. Whether they lost a job, or because of illness in body or mind, fellow beings must now live in the elements with their children and pets. We as a society too often consider them the "untouchables."

this journey

In tribal communities, all beings in the community knew they would have food and shelter if they took part in the tribe's work. When someone failed or got lost, the community would come together to support them, encourage them, have a ceremony to strengthen them. Today, maybe we stick a dollar bill out the car window so we don't have to meet the eyes of someone who hasn't fulfilled the requirements of our materialistic society.

I won't talk much longer about all that's not working, but I wanted to set a stage- as a tool to help you see how badly change is needed. Two percent of the US population has no shelter and 12.8% of the population has very low food security. One in seven children in the US live with hunger. 11 million children are living in food insecure homes.[4] World hunger is on the rise- nearly 10% of the world's population faces hunger daily. Whether war, climate change or global pandemics; so many people are suffering with really valid fear that they won't survive.

Yet, we have many people with more money than they could ever spend. They cling to their excess wealth, as they've been taught to do. Success is having tons of money. Success is living in the excess. Success is a big dang home, in the right neighborhood, full of stuff you may never use while there are others nearby without the basics to survive. All that money is insurance that the wealthy will never find themselves on the corner with a "please help" sign.

Okay, I'll get off my soapbox. The point is, we've been raised to honor the physical aspects of ourselves and of life. However, today, a new world has arrived. You don't see it on the news, but some of us feel it energetically. I noticed the first shift in energy in 2012, then another huge shift for me was Winter Solstice (North Hemisphere) in 2018. Everything started elevating for me. My healing work got more intense. My connection to others opened. My relationship to nature deepened. In 2020, we all plunged into a global pandemic, where we experienced the reality that money can't buy everything. The pandemic clearly reminded us all that our physical world focus is so wrong. Hoarding money or toilet paper wins nothing. I had a friend who had some income during the pandemic. I had none. She would buy family-sized baskets of sandwiches and sides and split them with me. She and I would chat in my driveway, always 10-12 feet apart, as back in the beginning we were all afraid of hurting and being hurt. I experienced living through the love and compassion of a friend.

Our upbringing in the old world taught us to value the physical- the money, the stuff, the fancy doo-dahs. We are now living in a new world. The energies have shifted. Some teachers share that we, as a collective energetically or spiritually, decided that it was time for the planet to elevate. Elevate means move to a higher level, a higher standard. Higher doesn't mean better, right-er as opposed to being wrong or evil. Higher is higher vibration. The shift is necessary as we've built a world that is not sustainable, fair, kind, loving, nor compassionate.

A world based on money and power is of lower vibration. In that world, we can justify wiping out so much of the Amazon rainforest.[5] We allow this devastation because it's profitable for some corporation. I live in a country where people lose their life savings to pay for medical care, trying to stay alive while the medical and pharmaceutical industries make astronomical profits. I could go on and on, but you likely have your own experience of how money is valued more than the welfare of our people, our plants and animals, our earth.

Prioritizing industry and profit as our god is not sustainable. Continual growth in size of business and profitability is not supportable. We as individuals can join the spiritual collective to say it's time for change. Love and compassion must be placed in power for us all to survive. We each must shift our thinking down from our busy brains to our heart centers and begin finding our compassion for others. We will change our world by changing ourselves, by becoming the love.

You might think, "Yeah, that will never happen" but it will. I don't know how it will happen globally, but individually the shift has begun. It's not a contemporary thing. There have always been powerful examples throughout history, pointing us to love. Jesus, Gandhi, Mohammed, the Buddha, Martin Luther King, Thich Nhat Hahn, and many others have shown us that the path to peace and prosperity isn't through war and destruction but through love.

Our old world used greed and fear to control the masses, so people will settle for devoting their life to grinding away at a menial job, forsaking their own power and purpose in life. Our purpose became to survive. Many of us are in fear of losing home or food. So we march on, serving our sentence, not dancing our own unique and beautiful dance.

this journey

"Putting food under lock and key was one of the great innovations of your culture. No other culture in history has ever put food under lock and key - and putting it there is the cornerstone of your economy.[...] Because if the food wasn't under lock and key, Julie, who would work?"
- Daniel Quinn[3]

There will be so many changes. Take a deep breath with me and say this out loud or to yourself, "change is needed, change is good." I don't know how our daily life will change as we move towards a more equitable, sustainable, loving world. Change will fix things. Change will lift us. Change will be hard. Try to release your fear of change. Life may look very different in the future. I trust that the differences will be good. I'm speaking to the "old world" part of you and me too, right now. In the new world, you might not have access to all the toxic products and chemicals we've gotten used to. You might not run your air-conditioning at full blast all summer long. You might not choose to waste water keeping your chemically treated lawn green all summer. Your front lawn might transform into a lovely organic garden of fruits and vegetables that you share with others whose gardens aren't as large as yours. Things we've considered "necessities" really are not. They are creature comforts. Remember, while you're running water down the drain waiting for it to feel warm enough, there are people all over the world with no clean water to drink. Things will be different. Relax, breathe deep and visualize a world at peace, not starving, not at war. I can give up some old world comforts for that gift. You?

When did we come to believe that humans are perfect and not in need of evolving? We have gotten used to the old world, but that doesn't mean that things have to stay broken forever. We are strong, intelligent, resilient people. We can learn new ways. The world cannot change if you and I are not willing to change ourselves. Who knows what might lie in the future that could assist this process, but for now, we are here to save the world with our love. Let's get to it. See yourself and anyone or anything that is part of your world as worthy of compassion and love. Remember that everything has physicality and spirituality, everything is visible and invisible, we all exist in ways that are practical and magical. Yes, all people have a higher self, deeper wisdom even if they're not tapping into these tools. All beings, even those people who piss you off and you wish to blame them for _____. All people are body and energy. All beings have a bright spark within, even if they are clueless or deny it.

I'm suggesting that even though the media might only share all that is broken, there is a fix. You can make a difference. Finding paths to love and compassion will change you. You are surrounded by loving energy when you make love your priority. Others sense that love energetically and respond accordingly. So choose to be something new in this broken world. Become part of the solution.

How can seeing and changing this broken world help you

You have all watched the energy of a room change when someone who is obviously having a bad day walks in. Everyone quiets, withdraws, puts up a wall or at least a boundary. The energy you allow to fill you affects you, primarily. Walking in fear and hopelessness about the state of our world keeps your body, mind and emotions in fight-or-flight mode. This is hard on your physiology and on your mental state. Take a deep breath and realize that in small ways perhaps, you can cultivate and express some hope, some love. Start with the easy places- love your pet, love a good meal, love a walk in the woods.

How taking action to shift this brokenness helps the world

Change yourself and see how that leads to change in how you treat others. This is the beginning of empowering our changed world. You are not alone in this work. There are millions of people globally who are seeking to lift our world. Daily, people are putting positive energy out, praying, visualizing, loving, which adds to the power available to help our new world become visible. We won't see all the results from our shifting to love and compassion in global ways, perhaps for decades. But living from love and compassion changes your life immediately and the powerful good energy that will shine around you will help all those nearby. Be the change.

this journey

The new world is here

We live in a transformed world. I know many of you say the world is changing, but I believe humans are hustling to catch up with our changed world. Most of us were born into the old world. That world focused on the physical, the visible, the practical/logical. If we couldn't see it, we weren't sure it existed. Well, except for radio waves, then television transmissions and then cellular? But mostly we wanted proof of everything. We want explanations and definitions. This wasn't always the case.

For all the wonders in technology, our modern world made one crucial change that is now being corrected with the arrival of the new world. In most tribal cultures, the spiritual or the sacred exists everywhere- in the plants, the land, the water, the weather and in each of us. This invisible, energetic aspect of life exists in all things. Our modern world took the sacred away and locked it out of the reach of the average human. We were told that we needed a mediator to engage with the spirit or the magic. While originally, we were perfect creations of the source of all things, some religions chose to teach we were by nature- dirty, wrong, lost, "filthy rags". However you define spirit or energy, the invisible, sacred world was now located beyond our reach. "God" was labeled male, given human weaknesses like jealousy and vengefulness and moved far away from us. Humans began seeking ways they might reach out to or please this god… to be deemed good enough. They were trying to connect to the sacred through others who promised to open the gates if we changed, gave money, thought as they thought. We lived in bodies that some deemed less valuable, or perhaps even a limitation or hindrance to finding a connection to the spiritual realm.

In our new world, I'd like to help erase that separation. In the new world, we can face and embrace the fact that along with the physical is the spiritual/energetic. Much of our world is visible, but there are also the invisible aspects. What is invisible is just as real and important as the visible aspects honored in the old world. Many aspects of the old world seem clearly practical or logical, yet some stubborn mysteries are just magical, defying explanation based on our understanding of the moment. Each being, plant, animal, drop of water is physical and energy. You came to this earth as spirit in a body. You are part of the holy, the sacred, the higher wisdom, universal consciousness, the source energy. So many of us feel that spirit is beyond understanding, but it is not. You are an aspect of the sacred. You are an intricate part of the source. You have access to the highest wisdom. We all are more than we know, whether or not we can feel that abundance at this point.

The old world, based on separation and fear, has turned out to be unsustainable, unfair, unkind, unloving, not compassionate, and often not satisfying. The powers of our cosmos, I'll label that the source of all things or the universal consciousness, called together all aspects of wisdom and together they decided that earth needed to elevate or it was a goner. So, the energy of this planet began elevating. I know this might sound woo-woo, but there are facts and science behind these ideas. I'm also comforted that many teachers in our world are supporting this vision. They might use different names and timelines, but many agree that the earth has changed to survive.

Changed to what? The old world honored money, greed, and a lust for power. Destroying the planet is okay as long as it's profitable. <u>This is not a good long-term plan!</u> The new world honors love and compassion. It is structured on a concept familiar to those in tribal communities. I am not suggesting we should return to tribal lifestyles, but in many of them, everyone had a place in the community. You performed tasks that were needed by the community, doing work that suited your interests and skills. You had food and shelter and were a part of a whole. In our modern world, we got very swept up in gathering things so we might never find ourselves in need. We hoard even if our neighbor is starving, believing that the other person isn't as important as we are. Truth is, we are all part of a community, a global community that includes all beings, all entities, all life. To me, that means plants, animals, trees, water, soil, people (yep, all of them), and ecology. Each of us is here to find our role, our place, in this vast community. We are here to serve, and we can do that with love and compassion.

There was once a world that honored money and greed, and controlled people by keeping them in fear. That world has shifted to one that honors love and compassion. All that remains is for us humans to get up to speed. If you have walked out the door every morning to a world awash in fear and lack of hope, it's hard to begin shifting your expectations to look for positive changes. But they are there.

I know it might sound strange for me to say the new world is here, but you can't see it yet. However, there is a phenomenon called inattention or perceptive blindness, which happens when an individual cannot perceive something because it's unexpected or unknown. I feel safe in saying that most of us don't expect to find love and compassion highly valued in our world, as those kindly actions have not been valued historically. Consider that the average person in the US takes in 70 minutes of news a day. (although that number does not include news read on cell phones, iPads, or other digital devices).[6] The news reports the events of the day, mostly bad news. This creates fear and a desire to know more. We feel that the environment is dangerous and we watch more to not miss out, to be prepared for what is coming. We keep watching, expecting the next awful thing that may come.

Humans have a negativity bias. They pay more attention to negative events, emotions, and news than they notice the good. This stems from prehistoric times, when not noticing what is wrong could mean you become lunch for a giant reptile. Today, media companies cater to our negative bias, showing us what we want to keep their profits high. So after consuming the the negative news, we walk out into our daily lives expecting more of that same bleak picture painted by the news. I found this study, which might seem a bit bizarre, but shows us how we only focus on what we are instructed to see. "Gorillas in our midst: sustained inattentional blindness for dynamic events" is a study conducted by psychologists Daniel Simons and Christopher Chabris.[7] They showed a video of three people in white shirts and three people in black shirts passing a basketball to each other. The viewer was asked to count the number of times the team in white shirts passed the ball to each other. Respondents reported their findings of 15-17 times. More interesting was when the viewers were again asked to just watch the video without counting, they then observed an adult in a gorilla suit who came out on the basketball court, pounded his chest, then walked off the court. The respondents thought they were watching a different video, however it was the same as they had watched the first time. We see what we focus on. We focus on what we have been told is important. So it's no wonder that seeing a new world isn't on most people's radar.

It might take a few decades until people can see and engage with this new world which values love and compassion, but we have a part to play now to make the elevation clear to more people. Our role is to change our thoughts and our actions to ones that express love and compassion. We each need to connect our physical self deeply with our spiritual/energetic self. It's time to still enjoy the visible, but know the invisible is here as well. While we might find comfort in the "same old" of the practical and logical solutions, welcome to the time of magic.

When the modern world took the spiritual, the divine out of each of us and placed "god" off in some faraway place, everything shifted. This is the time to shift back. Your ability to navigate, share and thrive in this new world hinges on you embracing your spiritual you, your divinity. I'm not talking about religion here, although celebrate yours if it brings you peace. What I am suggesting is to embrace the spiritual, invisible, magical part of you.

Embracing the idea of the new world helps you

As you choose to take loving and compassionate actions in life, you are surrounding yourself with positive energy. You know how when someone is having a bad day and they walk into a room? Everyone notices the shift in energy. This is one of those invisible aspects of life. When you choose to love, and you enter a room, people feel that positive energy and they are lifted a bit by it. You feel better and those around you feel better, just by small, loving thoughts or actions. It's good for your body and your energy, your visible and invisible, your practical and magical.

Embracing the idea of a new world helps us all

You might think that you, just one person doing small things, can't make much difference in the big picture. Remember you do not live in isolation. You are part of a global community and its energy. Imagine that you have a bucket of water. Your digital thermometer shows the water is 70 deg F. You drop just one ice chip into that bucket and while you can't feel a change in the water's temperature, your digital thermometer registers 69.9 deg. Drop a warm pebble in the same bucket and you find the temperature shifts to 70.1 deg. If you were the only being on the planet choosing to make loving changes, then the changes might only be sensed by your immediate family. But there are millions of people all over the world making these same choices. You're not heating that bucket of water all by yourself, and you're not solely responsible for creating a significant shift in the world's energy. You are responsible for working to help move the dial towards love and compassion. In time, the changes will be noticeable through the efforts of many of us.

this journey

Global awakening and emotional maturity

The previous chapters were pretty gloomy, but not gloom and doom. Until we really feel or see the brokenness, how can we fire up our passion to help bring change? Survival by focus on the physical is not working. How then can we fix the world?

May I propose we will not fix the world using the same tools used to build this broken one? The structures of government, religion, our medical care are all built from a fear-based system. It's time for something all together different. The change won't come down "from the top," meaning our government, or banks, or educational system. The churches do not have the abilities to fix this broken world. It's also important for each of us to let go of blame. "It's their fault" might feel like an action, but blame just disempowers you. When you do that, in a sense, you dust off your hands and feel you're off the hook. It doesn't matter who you feel broke our world. The point to discuss is if we can fix it? Yes, I believe we can. And it's <u>my job</u> to do it. Not just me alone, mind you. I will help fix the world. You can help fix the world. Each of us has a role to play. Step one is simply to move back from hate and blame. Lower your eyes, put your hands on your heart and take a deep breath with me. We will fix the world with love. Sound trite? Oh my goodness, no. I'm talking about embracing the power of love, taking action in love. It's an unmatchable power.

Maybe some giant magic wand will drop out of the sky and change the world. But I'm not waiting for that. I think the changed world is here. Yes, I've mentioned that several times, but I'm repeating myself to help reprogram your old world brain. I think that the new world is here, but we are so used to our normal state of brokenness we can't see or experience these elevated energies that are here to help us. We expect someone else to do something. We are waiting for the second coming of Christ or aliens or another war… what are you waiting for?

this journey

I'm trying this tack. When I was a child, and something went wrong, I expected mom and dad to fix it. I was just a kid, after all. I wasn't emotionally mature so needed taken care of. As a child and an adolescent, I had a "me" focus. I wanted MY things. I wanted MY way. I would take my toys and go home if things didn't go my way. I would want to stay home sick if there was something I didn't want to face at school. But I'm not that child anymore. Embracing emotional maturity requires that I embrace the power I have to help this world in need. Seeing my role as a true adult includes viewing my world truly, and seeing my role here to be of service to it, using my unique skills and wisdom.

> "Arrested personal growth serves industrial 'growth'. By suppressing the nature dimension of human development (through educational systems, social values, advertising, nature-eclipsing vocations and pastimes, city and suburb design, denatured medical and psychological practices, and other means), industrial growth society engenders an immature citizenry unable to imagine a life beyond consumerism and soul-suppressing jobs."
> - Bill Plotkin, Nature & the Human Soul: Cultivating Wholeness & Community in a Fragmented World[8]

Plotkin introduced me to the idea that, as a society, many of us are stuck at an adolescent level. We want our stuff; we want it our way- me, my, mine. In my understanding, Plotkin suggests that a true adult is someone who has dug within to see who they really are, who they want to be (purpose) then realize that they have a place in a community. The focus of our work is to help the community, not the self. I still have areas of life where my adolescent wants to be front and center. I must consciously tone down the childish part of me, turning to how I can most help my community and the world. It's about growing my focus from me to us. That's a big job.

Where to start if I'm to empower our broken world? I choose to embrace the power of love. We have delegated love to hearts and flowers, to romance and physical love in our society, but this love I'm referring to is infinitely more powerful. Robert Johnson[9] put it this way in "The Fisher King and the Handless Maiden."

> *"Sanskrit has 96 words for love; ancient Persian has 80, Greek three, and English only one. This is indicative of the poverty of awareness or emphasis that we give to that tremendously important realm of feeling. Eskimos have 30 words for snow, because it is a life-and-death matter to them to have exact information about the element they live with so intimately. If we had a vocabulary of 30 words for love … we would immediately be richer and more intelligent in this human element so close to our heart. An Eskimo probably would die of clumsiness if he had only one word for snow; we are close to dying of loneliness because we have only one word for love. Of all the Western languages, English may be the most lacking when it comes to feeling."*

How can you love this world filled with pain and violence? Easy! First, start by consciously loving the things you can love. Love your family, your pets, your garden. Dig deeper into what that love means. Focus on ways to express your love to those things you care deeply for. When you're frustrated or frightened, turn your attention to those you love and fill yourself with that loving energy. Stretch your love muscles, get familiar with the distinct faces and expressions of love. If my use of the word love doesn't resonate with you, try using the words value, honor, cherish, seek to preserve, or appreciate.

> *"The most important aspect of love is not in giving or the receiving: it's in the being. When I need love from others, or need to give love to others, I'm caught in an unstable situation. Being in love, rather than giving or taking love, is the only thing that provides stability. Being in love means seeing the Beloved all around me."*- Ram Dass[10]

Next, venture out with your love. Try loving things you feel ambivalent about- love your mail person. Consider how much work they do to make your life easier. I love the garbage collection crew. I smile and wave to them when I see them pass by and take my garbage away. Try loving your co workers. Love doesn't mean accepting unkind behavior, but try to find something worthy of love in those you spend your day with. Those beings aren't perfect, as you are not perfect. All are worthy of love, respect and honor at whatever level you can manage.

Do you love the trees, the flowers in the spring? Can you honor our planet, the ocean, the sky? Will you pause regularly and bask in their beauty and support? Try expanding your skills in love in these ways.

this journey

Breathe in the air with respect. Soak in the energies of the sun and the earth with awe. Fill yourself with positive energy.

When you feel ready, take a run at loving someone you don't know. That person might seem different or unfamiliar. You feel a sense of strangeness when you're near them. Notice people when you're in a crowd. Stand near a person who seems different from you- whether in race, size, or attire. Breathe in the air, the same air they are breathing, then offer them a smile and a kind look. Breathe out a bit of positivity to them. Each person, animal, plant, river, cloud and rock in our world has a wealth of ways they can engage with you.

Being loving never means that you accept abuse or endanger yourself. Love doesn't mean you ignore the pain others have given you. Love means releasing the power that past painful experiences hold over you. Try to accept that bad things can happen, but don't resign yourself or let that experience define you for a lifetime. And don't hold that one who hurt you as forever condemned. Don't allow them to hurt you again, but don't define all people who look or sound like the one who hurt you to be "bad" too. Find your forgiveness as another form of love and allow yourself to set the pain down and walk on in life. Dropping the pain of the experience can be a life lesson. You can rise above the past- wiser, deeper and freer.

As you become more familiar with seeing love, feeling love, being love, then you have more power to see that the new world is here. You will notice more and more people who are also being love. You might notice the sun beam shining in your window as being love. The ecstatic way your dog greets you is indeed love. Organizations working to provide clean water to those who have none. Yep, more love.

We have two choices of emotions in this life. When you live in a physical world, only valuing things and money, it's easy to live in fear that someone will take your stuff away. I am encouraging you to open to that other emotion, love. Fill yourself with it and shine it out. No one can take that away. Your light illuminates this new world for everyone.

Each of us reveals the new world in each loving act we share. We build the new world on love. No one will ever believe you or value you because you beat them over the head or threaten them. They will, however, see your love and want to be a part of that without you saying a word. In this awakened world, our means of power are love and compassion. Love and compassion are what will be valued, honored, and emulated. How will we fix this mess- with love and compassion. How can I forgive them- with love and compassion. How can I be more- with love and compassion. How can I find and fulfill my purpose- with love and compassion. The new world is here. Shine your light to see it. Be the love so others might see the new world ways and learn to be it too.

Choosing to love and serve this world empowers you

I understand that I'm asking a lot of you. I ask you to consider how you can shift your focus from fear to love. It's not something that can happen overnight. But every small loving step you take, every shift in perspective that you choose, you are freed just a bit more. The world will appear more lovely to you. You will feel that shift as it becomes easier for you to make the loving choice in all you do. People will respond differently to you. Synchronicities become more common. This isn't a magic wand of instant gratification, but in time, if you choose love, it will begin choosing you.

Choosing to love and serve changes the world

As you change how you engage with the world, you'll notice others with similar energy, similar purposes. You will find an affinity to organizations and businesses that you sense are also on this path. "Like begets like," as the saying goes. You radiate kindness and the person who received your sunbeam of love walks away and shines their light on others. There are millions and millions of people already in the world living this purpose. Add your light to this energy and, in time, the norm will shift and love will win.

this journey

6

New world- new you

Yes, I believe there is a new world here for us, but we don't readily see it yet. We certainly can see what is wrong with our old world. The news organizations make a lot of money by telling us 24/7 about the events that are going wrong in the world. I'm not suggesting you not care about strife in our world, but I do advise you not ingest a diet filled with bad news. We become what we surround ourselves with. When you pay attention to what isn't working or when you complain about problems, <u>you are giving your life force energy to the very things you wish did not even exist</u>. Think about the term "paying attention." You are paying with your time and your energy. Focusing your attention on the bad news empowers what is wrong and actually takes energy, hope and creative solutions off the table for you. To be part of this new world, we have to change. I suggest you explore ways to change by keeping your focus on the positive. Tune your attention to what is right as often as you can. What wonderful things can you imagine or visualize in a new, better world? Let go of blaming and see how the world can be different by looking for the positive, by building your hope.

Sure, take some time here to journal. Dream up a better world, visualize it, feel it and smile.

Now, I have another challenge for you. What role could you play well in this new world? What skills do you have that are needed in this new world? No one person is going to pick the world up on their back and carry it to some new existence. But each of us can lift ourselves, empower ourselves with dreams and visions that align with our strengths, and take action. Moving forward in love and compassion, using your innate skills and talents, are perfect ways to help this new world be more visible. Taking loving action empowers this new world, enables you, and generates a lovely aura of hope and love around you that lifts those nearby, whether or not they know you.

Part of the wonder of this new world to me is the energy of it all. When we embrace a physical and spiritual world together, then amazing energy comes into the mix. All I have to do is gaze at another

this *journey*

person, visualizing them in their perfect body/spirit balanced power and they are empowered. I don't have to say, "Hey, you should do this or that" I just treat others as the whole, complete beings they truly are. Whether or not the other person sees themselves my way, my interacting with their wholeness empowers them- physically and energetically.

"You lift others, not by denying them love, but by loving them more." ~Paul Selig, from the Guides[11]

I try to speak to others with my heart open and my spirit reaching out to theirs. Even if we're just talking about the weather, or discussing directions. When I do that, they walk away from the encounter feeling good, feeling more, feeling peace, love and compassion. This is the power of living connected to the visible and the invisible, the physical and spiritual, the practical and the magical.

How does this new world need you? It needs you to connect with the world, other beings, the plants, animals, water, air, the cosmos itself with love and compassion. And yes, I have to retrain myself on many levels to accomplish this regularly. The new world is asking me to be a grown-up, to find my place and serve the larger community. Do I succeed with this intention all the time? Oh, hell no! I falter, stumble, bumble my way through many days, but I am changing. I know I must change. Likely you know that too. So what the world needs now… is your love and your compassion. Imagine your role in this new, kinder world. Then practice living your way to fulfilling your new role. You can do this!

How living your role in the new world helps you

Just the simple act of choosing to focus on ourselves and others with love and compassion brings a relief, a lifting to us. In this positive position, we feel more hope, more power, more options. We can see a bigger picture than is possible when we focus on brokenness. You won't live in the positive perspective all the time, but perhaps reminding yourself, especially when you're feeling low, is a great way to nurture change.

How living your purpose helps the new world

While you see yourself as an individual being, energetically/spiritually, you are part of a much larger community. This community is global, even cosmic. Everything you do affects the overall energy. Remember the bucket of water example from a couple of chapters ago? You are a part of a global energy bucket or circle or field. Your positive actions put energy into this field. Even though you might feel tiny and powerless, your energy footprint affects the whole. And remember how many of us are here with you, creating more love and compassion to shift the energy of our entire community/world.

> *"The flapping of the wings of a butterfly can be felt on the other side of the world."*
> *- Chinese proverb*

this journey

7

Body + spirit = you

Most of us grew up in environments concerned only with our physicality. What do I look like? How do I dress? What sort of house and neighborhood do I live in? How are my grades? Am I pretty, strong, popular? What color is my skin? How much money does our family have?

What's the first question people ask you when you meet? What do you do? Where do you live? Are you married? Do you have kids? All questions about how we fit into the physical world. We tell our children, "Oh, you're so pretty, you're so smart, you're such a good girl/boy!" We gauge our success as a human by these physical traits. And if I'm not smart, or pretty or well behaved… do I still have value?

Today's changed world calls us to see ourselves as more than some physical expression of life. The focus on physical aspects only honors the outside of our amazing selves. Focusing on the material aspects of life encourages building bigger, better piles of stuff to express our value. Truthfully, your value has nothing to do with things.

Beyond the physical is the energetic, the emotional, the spiritual. The word spiritual is not referring to anything religious. I am speaking of that invisible, magical part of you that exists long after your body falls apart. So, beyond the body and our stuff, there is so much more.

You are physical and spiritual.
You are visible and invisible.
You are practical/logical and magical.

When you were born, a spiritual/energetic aspect of you jumped on board. My take is that your body and spirit together came rolling into the world with a distinct purpose. This eternal essence of you came with great wisdom, skills, and goals. That spirit waited to find the right "vehicle," your physical body, to come into the world to help at this transformative time. One of my teachers believes we should know that be alive on "schoolroom Earth" at this revolutionary time is a great honor. There was a long line of souls signed up to come here, but not all could be accommodated with a physical body. But you won the lottery! You are here in the flesh. So, can you doubt there's purpose for your "...one wild and precious life?"

"...Tell me, what is it you plan to do with your one wild and precious life?"- Mary Oliver[12]

When we value only the physical, we are continually seeking more. We ask our family, our mentors, our friends, our gurus... why am I here? What's this all about? We read books, get more degrees, find new gurus, yet are still unsure of our purpose, not confident in our next steps. Truth is, learning from others is wonderful, but your ultimate source of your truth, your purpose lies in your inner/spiritual self, nestled right inside that physical body of yours.

Each of us comes here with work to do. None of us will save the world single-handedly. Each of us has special skills, passions, interests that can allow us to help elevate our struggling world as no one other person can. Every person has a unique role to play. Perhaps your passion is ecology and you work to help save a species of turtle or you research how to get clean water to areas that are becoming more arid. Maybe your passion is animals, so you rescue dogs or cats and find them new loving families. Any of those "jobs" might not seem significant enough to save the world, but they are. Any action based in love and compassion is going to make a difference. Raising children to understand the importance and power of kindness and compassion is a fine purpose. But once those children are adults, how might you redirect or expand on your purpose?

As our world awakens, the new commodity we need more of is love. As you seek to help, choose to love and the energy from your life lifts us all. Remember how you can feel the negativity in a room when someone who is in a bad mood arrives? Your positive energy can lift a room. You connecting with your loving purpose will lift our world. When we live as just physical beings, we can feel lost and frightened. Same as if we listen to too much news, filling our mind with the negative aspects of the world today. When you connect your spirit with your physicality, you have a more rounded viewpoint and greater positive power in this life.

There are really only two emotions- love and fear. Too much negative energy keeps us fearful. When we wrap ourselves in fear, we are compliant and weak. We'll listen to anyone who promises to fix things for us, whether they are honorable or just out for their personal gain. As you embrace the power of love, you are actually maturing into the real you, the true you. When you release the addiction to fear, you have space within you to listen. With practice and patience, you will find there is a voice within you that is so wise and calm. You might find that voice more clearly if you focus on your heart area of the body or allow your attention to float down to the gut. Just breathe and listen.

You might say, "That sounds good, but how do I begin?" Honestly, keep reading, wandering on through this book. Each chapter is intended to open a new door to you, or expand some basic knowledge you already have. Take a deep breath and close your eyes. Notice what thoughts are floating around in your head. What thoughts distract you from your reading? What thoughts are familiar loops of thinking you often get caught in? Now, imagine your attention moves from your head down to your heart. I'm referring to the center of your chest, your energetic heart center, not so much your heart, the pumper of blood. Imagine the next breath in, you're breathing right into that area of the chest, filling it. Can you sense something different when you focus on your heart center? Some might notice feeling more calm, maybe more peace. Don't worry if you don't. But do notice now that those busy thoughts in your head seem a bit further away than they were when you started this exercise.

The action of changing focus from head to heart or to gut will often open access to a different perspective. Many feel that the heart or gut are connections to our higher self, our wiser self... yes, our spirit. Don't worry if you're not feeling the connection yet. There are many more opportunities coming. These ideas are practices- skills that build with time. As we get more comfortable with new ideas, you might feel a bit more awareness or connection to this higher version of you. Be patient. It is there.

this journey

Your higher self, your inner wisdom, your sweet intuition, that interesting hunch you had... all are voices of the spirit in you. You are body and spirit, visible and invisible, practical and magical. The body isn't better than spirit, the spirit isn't more holy than the body. The amazing power that comes to us as awakened beings is to allow the spirit to empower body and to allow the body to empower spirit. Your spirit needs the vehicle of the body to achieve the purpose you came to life for. Body allows you to interact with others, form communities, to build, share, touch, teach and love. You are physical and spiritual- two halves of a whole. Allow yourself to embrace all aspects of you. Help your body be strong and healthy, allow your spirit to lead you forward. Breathe and listen, receive, and in time, know.

How strengthening awareness and connection between body and spirit helps you

Developing your ability to connect to and hear from your higher self gives you an internal guru, if you will. When our world only includes things we can see and touch, we run here and there looking for some wise direction or someone to make decisions for us. In matters of personal purpose, your higher self is the authority. Others can offer you opinions and sometimes that information is helpful, but you are the ultimate authority on you.

How building awareness and connection between body and spirit helps the world

As we connect to our spiritual aspect, we also can begin to embrace the idea that we're not the only ones with spirit on board. Everyone has this higher, wiser self within, even if they're not aware of it or don't believe it. By the way, it is not your job to tell them. But when I interact with others, especially those I don't resonate with or agree with, I find it keeps me grounded in my higher self if I remember the other person is the same as me. I imagine I'm communicating with that spirit part of them and it helps me to stay in my wisdom. This spiritual aspect is in all things, even those we think of as inanimate.

Our physical self is easy to perceive as an individual, but at the energetic level, we are all connected. So even that person who you "love to hate" is related to you in the energetic sense. Just food for thought. We'll develop this idea more in later chapters. By training yourself to begin to see the world as connected, the old physical world of us vs. them becomes more disempowered. The borders we draw between this country and that become just a physical construct. We are all one in the spiritual sense.

8

Living in fear

So many of us have grown up with fear as our foundation. It is a deeply ingrained aspect of our modern world. Again, I'm not painting a "Woe is me" scenario. By clarifying the old world and how it has affected us, that knowledge becomes our launching pad for something better. I am hoping to help you grow from a fear-based life to a life filled with love and compassion.

Do you watch the news? I'm not judging, just asking. Try to take the role of the observer or a reporter for a minute and imagine watching your brain watch the news. What I'm asking is to imagine your brain sitting in front of a news broadcast. You're the wise adult, just standing back and observing the mind and the newscast. What energy are you receiving from the news and from watching your busy brain? Not all news broadcasts are the same, but often they carry a tone of urgency. The presentation tries to grab our attention and sometimes to sway our opinions. How does the news attempt to change our opinions? Often through creating fear. The media wants us to watch their station so that advertisers will pay them for commercial time. Because of the human's negativity bias, we get more pulled in by the bad news. It helps me to remember that news is a business, not a public service. I'm old enough to remember a time before 24 hour new channels, so maybe I'm a bit more sensitive to the news than you who grew up with news channels running all day and night.

The media wants us to have FOMO, fear of missing out. They feed us some "critical information" and promise we need to know these things and there will be more important stuff in the next hour, after hour, after hour. For some of us, the news feels like a source of information we must have. We feel like we must know what's going on in our world so we can be prepared... informed... worried?

The news is informing us mostly about what is wrong. The broadcast shares moments of people at their worst. It's taking us to the "dark side" in a sense. A negative report has the power to shift your personal energy by sharing its heavy or dense energy. What it the goal of the news? I think a viewer believes that the news wants to keep us informed. Truth is, the news is a business with goals like any business- to make money, sell ads, get viewers. It accomplishes its goals, but how about your goals? When you need information (not just on world events), consider how you might get insights that help you care for all the aspects of you- body, mind, emotions and spirit.

Where else might we get important information on our life paths? Friends, family, mentors, gurus, books, workshops- all can provide insights for us. All this information is helpful in some ways. We have to gather info, learn, grow and expand our horizons. There is a balance here that I want you to consider. How does information that comes from outside of us compare to information that comes from within?

We were raised in a world that teaches us to follow authority, to find an expert, to get more and more training because without all that, we might be uneducated or unwise. We do need an education to grow into functional adults. But with no higher education, are we stupid? Heavens no! I know many people with little formal education who are brilliant in their field. We learn in many ways and we all come with inherent wisdom, the wisdom of the higher self, the energetic spirit, the universal consciousness.

We are navigating a world unlike any ever known in recorded history. So much is changing. We are seeing the cracks in the systems we've been taught to trust. The fear-based world wants you to blame someone, but honestly, there are no bad guys in the global elevation process. Fear divides us, encourages us to isolate ourselves and distrust others. Still, we seek answers. We want knowledge to know how to fix our broken world. This knowledge is important, but it won't come from outside yourself. The knowledge you need to "fix" your world will come from within you.

Our old world built systems that valued money and power. Greed is rampant. We destroy our natural resources because it's profitable. We have built a world that is unsustainable, inequitable, unkind, unloving and lacking compassion. The news may fill us with fear that things are falling apart. I say, good. The old system is broken, and things that are broken do fall away. It's not all going to fall down overnight. But as time goes on, we learn more about how the pharmaceutical industry or our medical system, how our government or services intended to protect our health and well-being, are not trustworthy. The list of broken aspects continues to grow.

Take war, for example. As a child, I had this revelation (to me) that if someone hits me over the head, I will never want to follow them willingly. I will only want to hit them back. We will never "win" by trying to conquer others. Just because we take their land, the resources, their possessions, they are not ours and those "conquered" people will often wish we'd disappear and never come back.

I shared that opinion with someone and their response to me was, "That will never change." Fear paralyzes us in so many ways that we believe change is impossible, but that is not true. This world will change or implode on itself. So, I'm focusing on supporting positive change.

"Well, something HAS to be done." Yes, I agree and the thing that needs to be done is twofold. One, each of us must work very hard to live from our power of love and compassion. We must work to release our fear and greed. The new world, the one that is here (but we're having trouble seeing), is based in love and compassion. To see this new world, to empower her to be seen by others, requires us to operate on love and compassion. And yes, I know firsthand what a stretch that can be. Similar to our crumbling old systems, we cannot make this change overnight. But finding new ways to live with love and compassions is critical to helping us all thrive in changing times.

This change is most difficult and so very important. I don't know what mantra you chant to yourself to get through the day but one of mine in, "Find a way to love." This simple phrase packs a lot in. It is calling me to find a way to love it all… the people, the events, the animals, the all. Can I do that? Oh, hell no. But can I bring my awareness to finding a way to love it all as often as I can? Yes. Could we try seeing our planet and all its inhabitants as conscious beings- physical and spirit? Can I view all beings as worthy? Can I view myself as worthy? Might I seek to see the value and wonder even in those that frighten me a bit? Must I view our world as one of love? The answers are clearly yes, yes, yes and more yeses. So take a few moments and consider how can you work to instill love and compassion as your habit to help elevate our new world.

The other thing that we must do to bring positive change is to embrace that the true power in our world does not lie in the government, in money, power or things. Physicality does not determine the validity of everything. The power that counts now is truly wrapping your life in the connection to energy/spirit and your higher self.

All I'm asking you to do is to live from love and compassion and use your connection to higher self. How's that going to fix the mess we're in? It will fix the world in ways we've never seen before. The power that operates through love and compassion communicates with us clearly through our higher wisdom. It is here and now. We become players in the new world by operating on its frequency, resonating with the new values. Choose to be an example to others of new ways of living. I remind you that this world is physical and spiritual, visible and invisible, logical and magical. You are called to get more familiar with the spiritual, the invisible, and the magical. You'll find those aspects of our new world by living with love and compassion, trusting your higher wisdom.

There is no separation in this new world from the true power source. Whether you see source as a god, energy, the earth herself, your ancestors, the cosmos… you are part of all those things. You don't have to be educated more, find a better guru, get someone to bless you. You are it. You have true power. You are an intimate part of the source of all things. And as such, you will help lift the world and open the eyes of others to the wonder that is possible in this amazing time.

How does releasing fear help you?

When you focus on what you fear, you give that thing your energy. From a quantum physics perspective, you are actually empowering the thing that you wish would go away. Choose to practice keeping your focus on the positive. That choice empowers you. You surround yourself with love and compassion. I learned that FEAR stands for False Evidence Appearing Real. Some of our fears are just habits from long ago. Make new habits to empower yourself and the world. Find a way to love.

How does releasing fear help the world?

Many of the people you meet every day were raised in a fearful environment. Many feel that it's wise to be afraid, believing that fear keeps them sharp or ready. As you develop more strength to live in the new, loving world, that positive energy radiates around you. I believe that the elevating energy helps others see that fear is not serving them, more often it's holding them back. So, it's never my job to tell someone else, "Hey, just don't be afraid" but instead, I help create a world built on a feeling of safety and love. Others can then decide to rise above fear all on their own.

9

A higher path and empowering others

Have you ever had a conversation with a fresh religious convert? I'm not singling out Christianity, but it's the religion I have the most first-hand experiences with. A newly "saved" soul in the Christian faith is on fire with his/her passion for the newfound beliefs. Some denominations send out their new converts to evangelize, to share their passion, and bring more new souls into the fold. That's nice, perhaps for some. But for those of us not wishing to play a part in organized religion, a conversation with a new convert is painful. Nothing that person can say will make me wish to be part of what they feel so passionate about. In fact, if anything, the conversation makes me want to run away and hide. I wonder if parts or of this book will feel that way to some people. If so, sorry. Go hide with my blessings.

Through this book, I hope to share with you some unique insights, some simple truths. I'm not asking you to believe what I believe,. Just sharing my perspective in a simple way that I hope might open some doors for your growth, power and happiness. I hope you are finding some content that resonates.

That said, how might you share these ideas? Go evangelize? AUGH … NO!!! We have enough people hiding in fear. One of my inspirations comes from author/channeler Paul Selig. Selig published his first channeled book in 2010. I found him around 2012 and have been reading/listening to the books ever since. I find a practical message there that allows me to be a better me. I particularly resonate with his Guides' suggestion on how we might help others see a path to greater awakening. No, it's not by telling them what I've learned and insisting they buy in. (grin)

> "Every act born in love claims the self in love." "You lift others, not by denying them love but by loving them more." - Paul Selig, from the Guides[11]

this journey

We are human and divine, and so are all beings. When we interact with another, we should do it with an awareness of our own physical and spiritual self. Our energy of love and compassion comes through in our interactions with others when we maintain our awareness of our own higher selves. In addition, we remember that the other person has a physical and spiritual self. Even if we're just chatting about the weather, and even if that other person has no interest in their spiritual, invisible, magical self, the exchange helps elevate them. According to Selig's Guides, my seeing or honoring that higher part of others empowers that aspect of them. This means that without saying a word about enlightenment, I can help empower that person's connection to their energetic self. Perhaps it's oversimplifying, but it's like planting a seed that might sprout and enable another to find or feel that energetic aspect of themselves somewhere down the road.

We can choose to interact with others as though the new world is here. We can do that by honoring love and compassion. There is never a need to say, "You need to get into your higher self", which helps no one and is more like evangelizing. We can choose to embody love and compassion, and then we interact with others as our best self. We choose to see the other as their best self, even if they're not presenting themselves that way. Our interaction energizes that spiritual/energetic part of them, which influences the physical. Yes, actions in the spiritual or energetic realm change the physical world.

I hope to keep this book accessible to people with a wide range of perspectives. Just as I don't resonate when the reasoning gets too "far out there," I want to find explanations that help you in the physical and spiritual, the practical and the magical. This explanation is walking a fine line between those, I know. However, just as you can sense the mood of someone who walks in a room, the people you interact with sense the energy of love and compassion in you. How this energy connects with the other person's energy to activate their energetic/spiritual self isn't a practical, logical explanation. But it works. So just as Einstein had a problem with the concept of entanglement, because it didn't fit the common knowledge of physics of the time, maybe you can accept that holding a higher energy when working with others can help their energies rise higher. Are we reaching their higher consciousness, or does the higher vibration help them through entrainment, as does sound healing? For now, I'm going to just leave it there. I don't have a practical, logical explanation, but on the magical/ spiritual side, this approach offers great results.

So, when you interact with another, you seek the best in them. You talk with them as though they deserve love and compassion. Will your actions possibly affect that other at an energetic level? Yes, absolutely yes. And might this loving, compassionate interaction fuel a positive response in another at a spirit level more readily than if you preached to them about how they should change? Again, yes- totally and magically yes.

How does choosing higher vibration help you?

For me, just acting from my higher self, combining my physical and spiritual powers, I inherently have more power. I am directed by something more than my busy brain. My intuition, my gut sensations, my hunches are so much more clear. I can face life with a lot more effectiveness than if I stay just in my physical, old world self.

How does choosing higher vibration help the world?

People are hyper-sensitive about what you say, especially in these highly divisive times. To just interact lovingly with another, while seeing their higher energy self, empowers them. Their human defense mechanisms are not triggered. The more small interactions based in love we create, the higher the energy of our world. Each bit of loving care opens the path to seeing this new world that is truly here for all of us.

this *journey*

10

Now is the time and you are ready

As we learn to open to our deeper skills and purpose, it is so important to remember that "now is the time and you are ready." I first heard this quote from Lee Harris.[13] Lee is an energy intuitive, channeler, author, and musician. He has been sharing his wisdom and the direction from his guides for over 20 years. Lee had shared this quote for many years when I first heard it and thought, "No, I'm not ready yet." I saw Lee speak at a Conscious Media conference in Austin in 2018. He again talked about this concept and finally, at that point on my journey, I believed he was right.

The first half of the statement (now is the time) reminds us the world has changed and needs our help now to continue its elevation process. By elevation, I mean its transition from a world where greed and fear rule to this new world where our power lies in acts of love and compassion. However, the second part is a stumbling block for many of us.

Are you ready?

There are many signs to look for in determining if you're ready. Here are a few <u>things that are NOT required:</u>

- *People regard you as an expert in your field, especially your family.*

- *You have a pile of money with which to fund, travel and promote the work you wish to do.*

- *You have quit your full-time job or otherwise rearranged your whole life to devote yourself to this work of saving the world.*

this *journey*

The biggest stumbling block that many of us face is the feeling like we're not enough. Raised in a world of fear, you are unsure of yourself. I can't estimate how many friends, students and clients I've talked to over the years who hope to work with their true purpose once they've got one more certification or degree. Just a side note, Americans have a reputation globally as the people who have more pieces of paper proving their value. Much of the rest of the world has more faith in their knowledge and wisdom gained by living life.

This stumbling block kept me in its shadows for many, many years. I sometimes regret waiting, but I know now that I had plenty of life lessons to complete before I could feel whole and ready to step out of the shadow. But even now, my qualifications include:

- *College degree- 0*

- *Funded to do this work- $0*

- *Nationally known as an authority on my subject. Well, I'm working on that. (smile)*

I have a lifetime of living, stumbling and rising again. I've lost jobs, love, money and sometimes I lost hope. Like you, I had a job, meals to prepare, houses to clean, dogs to walk. Along with those lessons and "normal" daily life, I continued passionate study and training. It wasn't until recently that I could put the pieces of this life puzzle together to see the bigger picture. "Oh… that's WHY I did all that?" So I could be ready to do this thing- this book, these classes, these sound experiences, these workshops. And I've been doing all those things for many years, but all along, feeling that I'm not really ready.

I have always had passions to learn, to study, to find new ways to do old things. I've worked with teachers all over the world- in person, from books and online materials. I've shared healing skills, shamanic ceremonies, explored sound, meditation, breathwork and energy because those are all the things that heal me, that elevate me. I did all the study, travel, experiences because it's part of who I am, not because I would write a book to help more people. I did it because I have a thirst, a calling… because it's part of my purpose. Now, I have taken Lee Harris' call to action to heart and I am walking into my purpose, because I am ready.

So what is your job, your purpose? If you're not clear on the answer, start with what you are passionate about. How might you engage with others in loving, compassionate ways to share your purpose? Each of us must spend quiet time pondering and action time moving ahead to figure out how we might best help this world. You don't need to quit your full-time job or leave the family or make any other huge moves to begin. The key is to honor the fact that you are here, in a human body, with a hooked-up spirit onboard. You are here at a time of unprecedented change in our world. The world is rebirthing herself and we can help, each in our own small ways. You are part of the global workforce who came to earth at this time to be on the team.

Your job? It's your job to find that answer. I can't tell you what to do. Only your higher wisdom has that information. So, pause, breathe, and spend some time chatting with the higher you. Likely you have a general idea of why you're here. You likely are fulfilling your purpose at some level already. Listening to your higher wisdom with help you pull together a more detailed plan and your next step. That's all it takes. When doing soul elevating work, there are no guarantees, no 27 step plans. Just a hint, an intuition of which path is yours and a suggestion of where to start. Then… you start.

Now is the time, and you are ready!

How does taking action now help you?

Taking action is sort of a self-fulfilling prophecy. When I hesitate to move ahead, inertia keeps me still or stuck. It's hard to see yourself in action when you are hiding under the covers. Take action in small ways to begin your journey. That might mean just talking to a close friend about purpose, starting a blog or volunteering in a way that fits your purpose. Begin and you'll be surprised how your next steps come clear. We can't wait to see the entire plan, our whole life laid out before we take one step.

How does taking action now help the world?

Most people I know are on overwhelm about the state of our world. They are focusing on what they fear or who they blame. I try not to dive into those conversations with friends and family. Instead, I hope to live in a different way- be loving and compassionate most of the time and work towards my higher purpose. I create an energy that is noticeable by many, but beyond that, I am adding positive energy to our cosmic consciousness. My little loving actions added to yours and millions of others around the world can change things for all.

Malcolm Gladwell, author of "The Tipping Point: How Little Things Can Make a Big Difference", explores the concept of critical mass. The idea is when a powerful belief is held by 10 percent of the population, then that idea spreads virally. Scientists that tested the phenomenon at the Rensselaer Polytechnic Institute, in upstate New York, discovered, "Once that number grows above 10 percent, the idea spreads like flame."

> "Look at the world around you. It may seem like an immovable, implacable place. It is not, With the slightest push - in just the right place - it can be tipped." - Malcolm Gladwell[14]

Part two

Taking action

In part one, I explained simple enlightenment and explored areas that can hold you back from realizing that enlightenment is already in you.

The following chapters discuss areas of power I've worked in my life. They have made huge differences for me and for my clients. If you haven't considered yourself a spiritual explorer, some of these practices might not be familiar. If you drop into a metaphysical store or google these topics, you can feel like you're diving into the deep end of the pool. So, I'm offering basic explanations on many topics. I don't expect you'll want to dig into all this, but I hope you might find a few that resonate. Take those ideas you want to learn more about and dig deeper through the many resources available in our world.

this journey

11

Where it all started for me

It all started with rock soup and a willow tree space ship for me. I was a shy, middle child in a family that lacked healthy skills to express emotions and love. It wasn't a horrible childhood, but I felt lonely and over-looked. There were three of us and I would guess that all of us felt about the same. My parents provided for us- food, shelter, clothing, education, basic life skills to cook, build, grow and fix things. But I think neither of my parents had well-rounded role models to follow. We ate well, played cards, watched tv, hiked, played volleyball… so there was a lot of good. But I never felt loved, wanted, or valued. It's hard to learn to give what you're not sure you received.

What I remember as best about being a kid was freedom. My mom usually wanted us outdoors, playing, so we weren't underfoot. We lived in the country on a small parcel between two large farms, so there were acres to explore. I remember fondly carrying an old battered pan with me on adventures, selecting proper rocks and plants that I'd put in the pot for "soup." Do you know how beautiful most rocks become when they're immersed in water? Wow! Talk about transformation. I would wash the mud off them before they went into the pot because I wanted the water to be clear and clean. Leaves and flowers often landed in the pot too. I would stir them, watch them, and dream. I never felt lonely outside. And the mixtures in that old pot were so beautiful. And no, I never ate the soup. (grin)

When I wasn't "cooking", I'd grab a faded blue hula hoop from the garage and run around the yard in my spaceship. Sometimes mom would tie a kitchen towel around my neck because, of course, we all fly better with a cape. Eventually, I'd fly towards the mother ship, a large willow at the south-east corner of the lake. I'd climb that tree up so high. I could sit in those sturdy branches for hours, watching the lake, the bugs, birds, frogs, and fish. I remember clearly the willow leaves swaying in the breeze and a feeling of being gently rocked in the tree's arms. What did I do up there? I escaped.

Other days, I could just wander back in the woods for hours. We had what seemed like an unusual number of trees that had an odd bend in them, so I could shinny up the trunk to a short horizontal place (the horses back, you know), wrap my arms around that horses neck as the tree trunk wandered on up high. I always loved riding those tree horses. They took me on such adventures and rarely kicked me off. Another bit of play was to set fire to a small twig and write in the air, drawing shapes with the smoke and watching them float away in the wind. (Don't ask me where I got the matches and don't tell mom.) I would line stones up in the mud along our small lake so the frogs would have a place to sit. I would sit in the culvert under our dirt road and watch the water flow over the stones…the leaves drift by, knowing no one could see me in this secret place.

It wasn't until I was much older that began to see this play of a child as creating magic for myself. I was honoring those elements of nature that I found around me, engaging with them and becoming more for the interaction. Maybe they became more as well. I was seeing what others had no time to see. I spent my childhood conjuring up dreams, visions, rituals, fantasies, and companionship in nature. I forgot about nature in my early adult life. When my career started turning me inside out, it was nature that once again provided the nurturing I so desperately needed.

My journey began in 1953, but I spent the first 40 years of my life trying to be someone else. I tried to be liked, popular, worthy of love. I aspired to be successful, affluent, and powerful. While I achieved some of these goals, they weren't really my aspirations. They were what the world told me I was supposed to be.

As a young adult, I launched into a study of religion. Our family was atheist, and that's a hard path for a kid in a farm community because everyone went to church. I felt like everyone had a rule book for life but me. So I explored Christianity first. I dug into the Bible, studying different translations with dictionaries and concordances. I was really trying to understand the meaning of it all. I wanted that rule book to be clear to me, so I could become "all right," like everyone else, a success. While I didn't find a comfortable place in church, I continued studying other religions, tribal traditions, ancient legends. I was always seeking those common keys, threads or truths that helped people, helped life make sense.

My life all came crashing down on me around 1990. I found myself laid off on the same day the bank called to confirm my employment so they could approve the mortgage on my new condo. I had turned in my notice on my apartment, so in essence, I was unemployed and homeless. Seemed like a great time to try something new. I sent letters (yes, that's what we did back in the olden days) to everyone I knew in business. I explained I was seeking a new opportunity uniquely suited to my skills. I got one offer, and it landed me in Denver, Colorado. The job wasn't a dream come true. I learned a lot from the artist I was working with, but it was the environment that I really needed. Denver was full of energy and beauty. It inspired me in ways I never had known. I hiked all over the mountains. I took my first reiki class. I had my eyes opened in many, many ways. Synchronicities abounded and when I paid attention, these unique opportunities took me on a fresh path in life.

> *"Two roads diverged in a wood, and I took the one less traveled by, And that has made all the difference."* - Robert Frost[15]

Over the years, I studied reiki, sound and many other forms of energy healing. I have been deemed a master/teacher for over 20 years. I became a part of a *tiospaye*, a small family unit in Lakota society. *Ti* means "to dwell" and *Ospaye* means "part of"-and literally means to be part of a circle. With them, I learned and experienced life differently through their ceremonies and rituals… and with kind, loving, patient guidance. I was gifted with an old ceremonial pipe, making me a pipe carrier.

The "I want to understand the real truth" story went on. I expanded my studies in alternative therapies: bodywork, shamanism, channeling, plant medicine, ancient tribal rituals and modern research, which often confirms the ancient practices. I've studied meditation since I was 18 and followed that into yoga a few years later. Yogic traditions have taken me also into breathwork and the power of spiritual sound. More recently, I experienced *Hatun Karpay*, the Great Initiation of the Inca, which took me on a ten-day journey into the heart of the ancient Incan Empire. We conducted 10-12 hours of ceremonies each day, led by the Q'ero *Paqos*, helping us find harmonic resonance with the forces of Nature through sacred exchange, or *ayni* in their power places.

In the beginning, my goal with all study and exploration had been to "fix me". As time went on, it was more a thirst or a path… a purpose. When I was a child, I dreamed that someday I would have a long white braid down my back and I would teach others, helping them to thrive in the world by understanding the old ways. I thought I'd teach them gardening, canning and how to sew their own clothes, as that's what we did when I was a child. Those were survival skills that I somehow thought would be lost. Now, my teachings include much more than tending the earth and clothing the body, but those skills are still part of my life. Now, empowering your body/spirit connection seems like a survival skill in these transformative times.

So it was decades of synchronicities, learning, exploring and wonder that changed my life. I intend for this book and the experiences here to be your synchronicity that helps you shift to a new level or release what's holding you back.

I dream that to share my years of experience might really make a positive difference on your journey. Your solutions won't come when the world gets its shit together- your solutions, your wise direction, are within you right now. The wisdom has been there all along, directing you to things you love, to serendipitous connections and to lessons just like it did for me in my life. By explaining some basic practices, a skill toolkit, I hope to deepen your connection to your higher self, your spiritual side and help you fulfill your purpose and help bring this new world into view for more people.

It isn't about enlightenment for personal gain. We are well past the me-me-me times. Now our enlightenment is for us all, as a whole. Not all people will embrace this new world as I might, but we must still view all others as body and spirit, whether or not they know that. We must love them all, have compassion for them all. We must shine our light because our love, our enlightenment, will lift them, elevate them along their path. This simple enlightenment is for me, for you, for all of us to help our new world become a safe haven for all.

12

Labels we wear

Before we dive into finding and fueling your enlightenment, purpose and passions, I want to talk with you a bit about your opinion of yourself- in other words, your self-image.

"Knowing yourself is the beginning of all wisdom." –Aristotle

"Knowing others is intelligence; knowing yourself is true wisdom." –Lao Tzu

As we begin exploring within, it's very important to get a grip on why we see ourselves as we do. Self image is learned. A child's self-awareness of who they are begins developing at a very young age. They learn, through experiences, who they are- socially, academically and physically. Personal experiences with parents, family, friends, teachers can help form our self-image. A harsh comment from a weary teacher can lead to a lifetime of feeling like you're not very intelligent. Exasperated parents can say one unkind thing, and a child can cling to the idea that they're not worthy of love. Relationships reinforce what we think and feel about ourselves. We decide through these experiences at an early age what we are capable of or worthy of. We often carry these labels into adulthood.

Yes, think about that for a minute. You are operating with a deep set beliefs about your wonder and worth as a human being based on the judgement of a grade schooler? Yikes! Some of us have had therapy that helps us begin to peel these labels off, but the effects of growing into our adult life with limiting ideas can put some of our big dreams and passions in hiding.

This paragraph from "Waking Up" by Sam Harris[16] opened my eyes in a new way. Sam was describing his experience with MDMA when younger. I'm not proposing you need drugs to do what he is describing. I ask you to imagine feeling what he is feeling and look at whether you feel that way about yourself. He was talking about how he was looking at his friend and realized he really loved him. He wanted very much for his friend to be happy, "making his happiness, my own."

> *"I was no longer anxious, self-critical, guarded by irony, in competition, avoiding embarrassment, ruminating about the past and the future, or making any other gesture of thought or attention that separated him from me. I was no longer watching myself through another person's eyes."- Sam Harris- Waking Up: A Guide to Spirituality Without Religion[16]*

"I was no longer watching myself through another person's eyes"… that statement slammed into me. How much time do I spend wondering how I'm perceived- do I fit in, did I dress appropriately, am I too fat for this outfit, am I too old, do they like me, am I pertinent? Holy shit! With all that focusing on the other person's perspective, it's a wonder I ever got anything done. If I have these struggles, I'm guessing you do, too. So as we launch into finding our enlightened self within, there might be a bit of homework to do. We need to take the focus off what others think. May we begin to see ourselves more clearly and find ways to love ourselves as we are.

First, we look at ourselves with fresh eyes to really dig in and find our passions and purpose. We need to find what labels are holding us back. Here are some journaling prompts that can help you explore. This can be a process, so tackle one or two at a time. Continue reading, but don't lose sight of this aspect of really connecting to your highest self.

- *What are some labels you might have carried as a child?*
- *Can you think of labels that might have helped you survive?*
- *Do labels from childhood hold you back today?*
- *What are some things you think you can't do?*
- *What projects have you failed with?*
- *What are you amazing at?*

- *What are your proud accomplishments?*

- *What skills help you excel at work? Do these skills bring you joy?*

- *Cherished compliments?*

- *What might you love to do but it feels out of reach for whatever reason?*

- *What kinds of people does the world need to change itself? How can you help?*

- *Are there skills you need to be your best you?*

- *What do people think when they meet you?*

- *What do your friends or co workers think are your strengths and weaknesses? (This is a fair question to ask, if you wish.)*

As you take time to pore over any of these prompts that resonate with you, allow me to encourage you with this idea. Whatever happened to us as children, whatever labels we received- that was then. You learned lessons from life experiences, but you made it through them as well. You're all grown up now. If you have experiences from youth that you feel are holding you back and you haven't explored them with a therapist, I encourage you to do so. Sessions with a good therapist can help you hold on to your lessons, your power of survival, your abilities to thrive in spite of challenges. A therapist can help us peel those labels off and free us to see who we might like to be now.

Many of us have trauma in our past, from childhood or later on. Those experiences can affect us for life, but let tell you a story that shows this painfully well. I met a woman in a class and she invited me to lunch. I went and felt so sad because the very first thing this grown, adult, capable, interesting human wanted to share with me was that she had been abused as a child. She said it with such finality, as if saying that told me all there was to know about her. I did not know what to say to her. All I could think to myself is "and then what?" I didn't say that, as I didn't want to sound like I was not taking her experience seriously. I have abuse in my past and only those closest to me know that. I sought counseling and then went on with life. That experience is always part of me but never defines me.

I think trauma is like a car wreck in a way. It's awful, frightening, and sometimes we bear physical and emotional scars from it for life. But we drive again. When we meet someone, I don't think we lead with, "Hi I'm Suni and I crashed the hell out of my car once." In time, we grow past the terrible incident, learn what we can from it, make provisions to avoid another crash and then march on through life.

The life experiences that affect our self-image negatively need attention and healing. But first honor and cheer because you survived! Something unthinkable happened, and you survived it! You rose above it and marched on with your life. I try to seek what lesson I can from the life's most challenging experiences. I have learned to see those who harmed me as humans who made really poor choices, but often, by the end of their lives, they also did some good, and likely they learned their own lessons.

Don't be like the woman at lunch. If she introduced herself to me by sharing what might have been the worst time of her life, I can only imagine how that label affects how she walks through life; how she might see herself as less-than powerless, or worthy of pity. Regardless of your label, don't make choices as an adult about what is possible for you based on ancient history. Some labels are based on actual events that happened. Others result from a teacher, parent or friend just using a wrong word at a wrong time. Neither situation needs to hold you back in life.

Humans have that negativity bias. Someone could talk to me for ten minutes, complementing something I've created, but if they say one thing that's not totally glowing, even constructive criticism, my human nature will focus on that less than perfect comment. This is part of a survival skill left from prehistoric times. In those times, when you walked outside of your cave, there were things that wanted to eat you for lunch- literally. We are wired to look for danger, to look for the off thing, the wrong thing, to keep ourselves alert and ready to run for our lives. Modern times have transformed our lives, so we might want to let go of this negativity bias a bit. Focusing on the negative is something we do but also is something, when aware of we can change. Or at least we can learn to recognize in ourselves.

I would never suggest that the hard experiences of life aren't important, but we made it through those times. What others said to us, or did to us, should not still be holding us back now. We can identify with the lessons and move forward. No labels, no limits.

If you're inclined to journal about labels you carry, do that. I want you to know that your self image could represent the perception of a 10-year-old child, created as a survival tactic. You're not 10 any more. Today you're dreaming about thriving, so help yourself peel these labels off.

Power of releasing labels for you

Every day brings us new information, new connections, and new ideas. Releasing old labels from our past opens new doors to us, drawing in fresh opportunities. Releasing perceived limitations allows us to see strengths that we were unable to see when plastered with those old limiting labels.

Power of pitching out labels for the world

Realizing that your own limiting labels are releasable allows you to consider that there are many others in the world, people and principles that we label. These people are good, those people are bad. This country is the best, that country is horrible. This church, this club, this political party… all gatherings of individual beings covered with labels. Each human in this world is very much like you. They want peace, safety, food, shelter and love. See beyond the labels. Look in each other's eyes and be surprised to find real, breathing, imperfect-but-worthy-of-love humans, just like you.

this journey

13

Your bright sparks from childhood

When I ask you about your passions, I imagine your face lighting up and your eyes sparkling. People are often happy to talk about the things they feel passionate about. Our strongest interests/affinities are a place of powerful connection of our four aspects- our mental, emotional, spiritual and physical selves. These strengths/passions came with us into this life for a reason, to do something specific. Don't worry, you are doing it. You are living with purpose. But can there be more- more power, more passion? I think yes, so let's explore.

Before we begin, I also want you to consider two things.

1. Are these passions focused on building or tearing something down? I ask that now, because we live in a world that has made a pastime or even a sport of divisiveness. Some people see their passion as being against someone or anti-something. We are a society that loves to hate, if you will. So first, the passions I want to hear about are things you love, things that lift you up, inspire you, allow you to get lost for hours in your happy place. Okay, breathe deeply, and ponder those sorts of passions.

2. My second question is, when in life did you develop this love? Just curious

So, what are your passions? Yes, grab that journal and make some notes. Likely you'll continue this exploration through-out the rest of this book, but for me, writing fresh ideas as they come helps me so much. Those quickly recorded light bulb moments have been keys for me in beginning to understand the story of me.

Before I babble on about passions and their power in our lives, allow me to first address those of you who are hanging around the back of the crowd in this discussion. (We ARE having a discussion, you know. How boring would it be for me to babble on and not give you time to reply? Smile.) Some of you don't have a quick answer when I ask about passions. I first want to talk about how it feels to be passionate or passionless, and then we'll explore ways we might identify our passions.

Some folks tell me that their passion is sports, then fill me in with details about their favorite team. I'm not doubting the quality of their love for their team, but I wonder how they take part in this passion? Do they watch the games, yell at the screen, bundle up and go watch a game in person, enjoying some adult beverages and less than healthy food? If this is you, just take a moment and evaluate the value of this passion. Is it feeding your soul or just keeping you busy?

Some tell me their kids are their passion. That's wonderful, of course. We all should love our kids, our families. When children are small, their care and feeding is overwhelming, especially for moms or single parents. But as they grow and begin leading their own lives, where do you funnel all that energy and focus that was once needed when they were small? I'm not suggesting that kids aren't a passion but want you to consider something that might bring you additional joy after the kids are grown.

If your answer to my question is unsure, "Well, I like to cook? I like to play video games," then we're not getting to the depth of passion that I'm seeking. If your passion didn't come blasting out of you in all directions when I asked about it, let's try this approach… what did you love when you were little? What did you dream of growing up to be? What roles did you act out in play? Just dial back there to childhood and ponder for a minute. Yes, time to journal some more, if you wish.

I do know that childhood wasn't a good time for many of us. But beyond what was wrong, there were still things that were right. My childhood was difficult for me in some ways, but I learned to entertain myself. I learned to be creative. I spent time in nature. I loved to draw. For this discussion, take a deep breath, release the painful stories of childhood (that I hope you have already discussed in depth with your therapist) and move onto what made you grin when you were little.

Your bright sparks from childhood

Each of us came into this world with a purpose. When we find knowledge, skills, activities that resonant with that purpose, we light up. Often, your life purpose is connected to the things you loved when you were a child. So, make yourself a cup of tea, or take a stroll to meditate on what you loved in childhood. Children are more free with creative activities than many of us are as adults. Can you remember a time when, if someone offered you crayons and paper, you always jumped onboard as an artist? Did you have pets as a child? Did you garden with your parents, or enjoy walks in nature? Did you dream of being an astronaut or a firefighter? Turn your mind back to those bright thoughts and dreams from childhood. Make notes in your journal of any fresh insights you might find.

Ahh, I hope that was sweet. Now, back to today. What did you learn? Whatever you dreamed of as a child doesn't have to be exactly what you do as an adult. If you dreamed of being an astronaut, you don't need to quit your job and head over to NASA. These passions we're reaching for don't have to be your day job. My hope is that you can use the positive energy of your passions to inspire and empower you as an adult. Rather than becoming an astronaut, perhaps you might check out local astronomy groups, or shop for a telescope. You might just take an hour out on the patio to learn (or relearn) the names of some favorite constellations.

A small firefighter might grow up to be of service in other ways- mentoring or volunteering to help people rebuild their lives after a disaster. A budding artist might carve some time out in the schedule to break out the crayons or paints, or offer to teach creative workshops to help others express themselves visually. A little ballet dancer might join an adult dance class or a folk dancing group. That dancer might also learn folk dances and share at a senior center.

The goal here is to take those sweet, energizing passions and allow them to add to your life again today. When our passions are engaged, our lives have purpose and so much more power. Our passions have a deep connection to our heart and to our spirit. We're strengthening those connections by exploring passions. So, turn off the TV, stand up and start moving toward your passions.

Power of loving purpose for you

With purpose more clear or blazing bright for some of you, let's explore how to bring that passion into your life if you are not already? Is there time every week devoted to your passion time? Are you still learning about your passion, or maybe learning is your passion? Mine is. Consider the expression of your passion. Instead of learning about styles of painting, are you painting? If travel is your passion but your budget or responsibilities don't allow time for it, then travel to the local park to explore. If creating music is your passion, are you sharing it? In our world, there are myriad ways to share our passions, online and in-person. You are ready, and it is time. The world needs you.

Power of passionate purpose for the world

When you express your passions, you are sharing love. You are excited about something positive and radiating that energy out. You might have noticed that many people today are in the habit of gathering together to complain, blame, or be fearful. Shine your light to help lift some of that fear habit. There are bright places in our new world today. Sharing your passion is one way you can lift others to see that there is love, hope and beauty in our changed world.

14

Learning to be the observer of your mind

We're beginning to explore within- wandering through childhood, choosing how to view past challenges. Seems like the right time to dig deeper into how our thoughts work and how we can learn to manage or direct our thinking.

Meditation is a simple and powerful tool to find calm, connection and space to hear your higher self. It is a natural state for all beings. Meditation is not stopping your thoughts AT ALL!!! This is the big misconception for most people. Stopping the mind is possible if you have practiced meditation for many years. Some people have a natural ability to put their mind in neutral. For some, stillness can be intimidating. So open your heart and mind a bit. Meditation starts with just watching your thoughts.

Take a deep breath. When you're ready, let it out slowly and notice what's going on in your head.

This is not a test, we're just practicing. So there's no wrong experience here. No one is going to judge you for what whacked out thoughts might fly through your brain. Just notice. Then let that focus go.

Take another deep breath. In 1…2…3…4 pause, let the air slowly out 1…2…3…4…5…6. Again, just take notice of your thoughts.

I imagine your thinking touches on some of these popular topics. "How long do I have to do this," "I don't have time for this shit," "Where is she going with this crap," Or, you'll find the ever popular thoughts like, "Oh god, I can't believe I did that stupid thing in front of all those people yesterday. I'll never live that down. They all think I'm a moron." Or something like, "The doctor's office called. That must mean something is wrong… really wrong… horribly wrong!! AUGH!!!!"

Maybe you can identify with some of these thoughts as you glance at your own mind. It is really quite normal to have fleeting thoughts about many things. Replaying the past or projecting the future are normal too. Mindfulness is the term used when we try to keep our thoughts in the now. Now is the only time you really have to take action, to live. Now is the time we can change, learn, grow, teach, touch, hug, live, love. Now is the jam. You have no power over what happened yesterday or what will come tomorrow. You have immense power in this moment, in the now. Mindfulness is a style or a tool of meditation. It asks us to keep our attention in the now more often.

One more important aspect of keeping your attention in this moment is that right now, you are fine. What? Yes! You are fine. Take a deep breath and go with me here for a moment. Right now, you are reading a book, so I might surmise that you are safe, sheltered, reasonably comfortable. You are likely clothed and fed. Hopefully, you feel loved. Right now, in this moment, you are okay… fine… great! Years of working with meditation groups have given me lots of feedback from making this statement. People want to tell me that they are not okay! Their relationships are awful, their kids are making them crazy, they have a medical condition. All those things can be true, but regardless, right at this moment, you are still okay. Your partner and children might need some work or a bit of space. Your medical condition may change what your future looks like, but at this moment, you are fine.

It's a stretch for some of us to realize that you can be okay, even if every aspect of your life isn't as you wish it. French monk Matthieu Ricard has written that happiness is "a deep sense of flourishing that arises from an exceptionally healthy mind."[17] Meditation asks us to understand that each of us has this healthy mind. Our minds might have some habits that leave us feeling confused by unnecessary or untrue thoughts. This is something you can work on. You may not arrive at Ricard's state of deep flourishing every moment, but there are skills we can develop which allow us to redirect unhealthy thinking and relieve stress.

Think about your normal day. How much time do you spend with your mind spinning tales about what was or what might be? Research shows we spend roughly 47% of our day thinking about something other than what is right before us, what is going on at this moment.[18] Sometimes we are reliving the past's sweet moments, but honestly, many of us replay the crap. We rerun the awful, clumsy, uncomfortable moments again and again while chastising ourselves for not being more perfect. Or we worry about what's coming. Will I be okay? Will my family be okay, my job? This can go on and on. Think about your thoughts for a moment? Have you had times when your mind seems to run off with you? Generally, the mind is in the past or the future when it imagines the worst. You can get so caught up in its flurry of thoughts that you feel it physically, experiencing rapid pulse, tightening muscles, clenched fists.

We all have thoughts that are triggers for anxiety. Some call these thought loops or circular thinking. We replay the same situation (real or imagined) over and over, while our stress and anxiety seem to get higher. We feel panicked, out of control. This is unpleasant but a quite normal situation. Mindfulness practices can help us learn to stay in the moment and become an observer of our thoughts. Watching our thoughts can help us learn to put a feeling of distance between us and these thought loops.

So let's take another look at your thoughts… where are yours headed right now? Imagine you're a reporter, just observing the thoughts. A reporter filling us in on a big storm just shares the facts- this much wind, rain, time until it's over. They want to share information with us, not induce panic. Try taking on the role of the observer of the weather in your brain.

Breathe in 1…2…3…4… and then let the air out 1…2…3…4…5…6… Just notice your thoughts…where are they headed? Just take note, "Oh, there I go worrying again." Then call your thoughts back to this moment. Take a deep breath. Keep practicing being the observer. In your imagination, consider taking a step or two back from your busy thoughts. In time, you might consider the idea that if you can watch your thoughts, then you are not your thoughts. You are something separate from your thoughts and this is a big Ah Ha for some people.

Many people feel as though they are their thoughts. When the thoughts get so crazy, folks feel as if they can do nothing but hang on for the ride. Thoughts are just thoughts, like clouds in the sky. They float by or run in crazy circles, but they're just thoughts. Small bursts of electrical energy that your brain translates for you. Your thoughts, your mind, are a sort of onboard computer. The mind serves as an important tool in life. Without your thoughts, you might not remember to go to work, know not to wear your PJ's there, and remember to send your mama a birthday card. Be grateful for the thoughts, but you are something separate from them, watching them, gently calling them back to the present moment.

Take a deep breath and remind yourself that you and thoughts are separate. Let's call you the observer of the thoughts. As the observer, you have a bit of separation from your thinking. It's like getting sucked into your smartphone. You can get lost in there for a long time. At some point, you snap out of the trance, plug the phone in to charge, and walk away from it. Your phone is over there, doing something, but you are in another room, being you. Meditation is like that. It gives you a path to pull the plug on circular thinking and get back into the present moment.

As the observer of your thoughts, you have the ability to notice when your thinking heads towards worry, for example, but you don't have to dive into the worry pit. You can stand apart from your thoughts, notice the unhelpful thinking, and then call your mind to something else. I often speak to my mind like it's a 3-year-old child I love. "Yes, I hear your concern, but that matter isn't in our control. Let it go for now and we'll go take a walk."

So take another deep breath- 1…2…3…4… and then let the air out 1…2…3…4…5…6…
Just pay attention to your breathing- slowly in, a bit more slowly out if that feels okay. Receiving fresh air and energy on the inhale and letting go of what doesn't serve you on the exhale. Did your mind wander yet? When it does, take notice of what drew its attention, make a note of that, then gently call your mind back to the task. "I hear ya, buddy, but right now, we're paying attention to our breathing."

We are learning to separate ourselves, our identity, from our busy brains. This is an amazing, powerful tool and is the beginning of meditation. Some days, all I can manage after years of practice is to call my mind back to now- again and again. It is perfectly normal for your mind to wander off from meditation or calming or whatever… writing this book. The mind can interrupt your practice every couple of seconds. That is not failure, it is NORMAL. You notice that your thoughts have wandered from now, from your breathing (from my writing), then call the mind back to the task at hand. That is success!!

As you begin, your mind might interrupt your calming moments over and over again. Remember that with practice, this will change. You aren't failing at meditation, or calming or writing… you're just practicing a new skill. You are learning to wrangle your mind and that, to me, is what meditation is all about. You are becoming aware of your body and mind. You are learning to "drive this car" of body, mind, emotions, and spirit. It comes in time. Just have fun exploring.

How does becoming the observer of your mind help you?

As I practice being the observer of the mind, I build power to direct my thoughts. Once, I might have felt unable to stop the crazy thoughts, but now I can. In time, I intercept unhelpful thinking as soon as it begins. Instead of seeing these triggering thoughts as giant monsters that will render me unproductive, I eventually can see triggering thoughts as nagging little habits. Learning to redirect our thoughts is very empowering and saves us so much time and energy.

How does becoming the observer of your mind help the world?

Being the observer of my thoughts helps me think more sanely and calmly. I could start telling the world, "Hey, quit thinking like a madman," but that's never an effective path. We can, however, choose to be a calm voice in any conversation. We can step back from another's thinking just as we observe our own thoughts and not get sucked into someone else's emotional rant. I find so many of us are feeling hopeless and frightened in the world today. Taking a deep breath and calling another's attention back to this moment might be helpful. Do this gently, with love and compassion.

Visit the website for online meditation resources. SuniMoon.net/readers

this journey

15

Aspects of consciousness

Let's talk about your mind and two of its personalities- the ego and the intuition. As with all topics of discussion here, I'm taking a practical, basic approach to a topic that is deep and wide.

We just explored watching our mind by playing the role of the observer. For some, this idea that you can watch and redirect the mind is unfamiliar territory. Some feel that whatever thoughts are flowing through their minds define who they are. As if you have "crazy" thoughts, then you must be crazy? Oh, my no! All sorts of thoughts run through our minds. We are not just our thoughts. There is so much more to a whole being. Truth is, we are our most powerful when we engage all of ourselves- our body, our mind/thoughts/emotions and spirit. The observer is part of our spirit, energy, our magical self.

Consciousness is defined as the state of being awake and aware of one's surroundings, the awareness or perception of something, or the awareness by the mind itself and the world.[19] There are three aspects of your mind or your consciousness - the conscious mind, the subconscious mind, and the super-conscious or higher mind. Let's begin with the most commonly discussed aspects of the mind- the conscious and subconscious minds.

The conscious mind is that mind we've been watching, the thinking mind. Some might call this our ego. This aspect of the mind is where you contemplate, problem solve, make choices, plans, or shopping lists. The conscious mind is also that place where you will replay uncomfortable events from the past and will worry about the future. The conscious mind is the thinking we are aware of. Some believe that work of our conscious thoughts account for only about 10% of who you are, what you decide, your behaviors and perceptions of life.

Beyond the conscious mind is the subconscious mind which holds your beliefs, perspectives, expectations, and fears. You may not be aware of the contents of your subconscious, but it holds the information behind the other 90% of how you think, react, and behave, why you make the choices you do, and the way you perceive life. You might not be aware of the contents of your subconscious mind, however, you can learn about it and shift it.

The subconscious mind's job is to keep you alive. It does that by keeping you on familiar paths, doing what you have always done again and again. The info in your subconscious comes when you were a child. Many believe that until the age of seven, a child cannot effectively tell what is true or not. A child absorbs what they believe are the actual truths of life from watching people they love and from their own experiences. What is around them is all a child knows of the world. Those experiences go directly into the subconscious as the truth of life. Children are born with only two natural fears- that of falling and of loud noises. All the rest of your fears you learn from these early life experiences.

Changing the contents of the subconscious happens first through awareness. Often a session with a good therapist can help us discern our deeply held beliefs that might need changed. For example, if you were raised in a violent home with parents who treated you poorly, then as an adult, your subconscious believes those experiences are the whole truth in the world. While your conscious mind wants you to be treated well, you find sometimes you accept poor treatment as an adult. Awareness of these old beliefs and adopting new practices can help us reprogram our subconscious mind.

I made that sound simple… all you need is awareness. Whoa! Awareness is step one, but to modify the subconscious mind takes work You are changing a deeply held belief, which is very much like building a new habit. If you've tackled changing habits, you know it's a serious undertaking. I've ditched many unhelpful habits in my life. I quit smoking. Hooray!!! I stopped using alcohol. Hooray! Hooray! Hooray!! (That one took three times to get it to stick.) I still struggle with addiction to sugar and am currently working on moderating that behavior. Just sharing, so you know I understand it's HARD to change habits but it is so worth it.

Our subconscious belief system is deeply ingrained. Once you identify a belief that you wish to change, then the work begins. I started working with a therapist and a support group for addictions. I used hypnotherapy to help stop smoking. I read and read and reread many, many books. I'm not even going to recommend one book on changing habits here, as new ones are released often. Ask google, a friend, or your therapist for suggestions. The plan of action for me is to repeat and reinforce and affirm the new behaviors/beliefs. Stick notes on the bathroom mirror and on the car dashboard. Put a reminder on the home screen on your phone. Schedule time every day to repeat helpful affirmations or read inspiring books. Journal, so you have a record of your progress in reprogramming old habits. Write when things go wrong. Write also what you might do differently next time. Write in that journal when things go right. Write when you feel like your new habit has really kicked in. Bottom line for me is to be kind to myself, keep learning and try, try again. These things take time.

Remember, your deeply held beliefs about yourself are the perspective of a child. If mom was having a bad day and screamed at you, "Can't you do anything right?" That incident may have engraved itself deeply into your subconscious… "I never do the right thing. I can't trust myself to do the right thing. I'm flawed. I'm not valuable. I'm wrong." Those negative thoughts are likely not top of mind for you. But when you dig into some of the journaling suggestions from the chapter on labels, you might have gotten some clues. I was a very successful corporate executive who felt like I was a fraud, just trying to avoid discovery. I never would have said that out loud back then. So relax when you explore these old beliefs. Remember yourself as the child who formed those opinions. Approach that little child part of yourself with love. You're an adult now. You can lovingly explain how the old misconceptions aren't true to your child self. Always be kind with yourself, knowing you will probably explain this new info on your value to yourself again and again. It's the process. You can do this.

Our super-conscious or higher mind is something different, perhaps not of the brain but rather of the heart, gut, or spirit. There are many names for this aspect of ourselves- the higher self, inner voice, spirit, higher wisdom, or intuition. Some people are more comfortable when contacting higher wisdom to think that they are contacting their guides, angels or god. Use the description that fits and works best for you. However you view it, you can connect to all wisdom, love and knowledge by seeking this aspect of yourself..

When I am acting as the observer of my mind in meditation, I believe I'm in that higher wisdom role. I can, as this higher version of myself, watch over my thoughts and redirect unwanted thinking. I can choose to pause when my thinking gets too rushed or painful. In that pause, with maybe the help of a deep breath, I can remember that my busy thinking isn't the ultimate authority. I like to shift my focus in thinking from the head down to my chest or gut. I take another breath. I remember thoughts are like clouds in the sky and painful thinking can float on by if I allow it. I then turn my attention to my breath, to this moment and often, a bit of peace, space, or wisdom arrives. We'll dig into this aspect of ourselves more.

Benefits of understanding and exploring the levels of consciousness for you

For me, these practices helped me expand my power. I'm not a victim of my busy thoughts, nor am I under the control of beliefs held since childhood. The mind is understandable and able to be changed. You can teach an old dog new tricks.

The power of practicing meditation gives us many opportunities to use the skill of redirecting thought. We are not the victim of our over-wrought mind. Taking a deep breath and turning our attention into this moment gives us a wonderful way to calm ourselves. Taking some time gives us a chance to choose our next action rather than just reacting. Remember, you have a healthy mind that is capable of "a deep sense of flourishing."

Benefits of understanding and exploring the levels of consciousness for the world

All beings are very much like you. Their thoughts get too busy and carry them off. They operate on subconscious beliefs that they learned from parents who were doing the best they could at the time. Society doesn't always approach each other with kindness and compassion… but you can bring that change. Caring for your yourself, learning to connect with your higher self brings a kinder, more loving you to the world. Every interaction you have can help one person and then that one person can help another. Remember, we are part of a global or cosmic community. Be the good neighbor, the helping hand, as you navigate life.

16

Connecting to your body

When we seek to explore the spiritual or energetic aspects of ourselves, it is not uncommon to feel that learning and change is all about mind and spirit. We can feel like floating heads being carried around by a disconnected-feeling body. Truth is, we are our most powerful when we engage all of ourselves- our body, our mind/thoughts/emotions with our observer/spirit.

Each being in our world is physical and spiritual, visible and invisible. We have strength and abilities in our bodies and minds, with unique powers in our spiritual aspects. Some religions teach that the physical part of us is flawed or less than, while all things spiritual are perfect. Our materialistic world might have helped you believe that your body is too big, too old, not "right". May we learn to value our body, just as it is. I believe that the spirit needs the body just as the body needs the spirit.

Your invisible self doesn't have the power of direct, audible communication. The spirit can't wrap its arms around another being and offer comfort. Our bodies have a wealth of emotions to deepen our experience of life. When we consciously connect our spirit with the body, the way we can see and feel life expands even more. The two aspects of ourselves- spirit and body, are more when together than they can be as separate aspects. When used in union, we can live as more balanced, peaceful whole beings.

So as we wander thru this exploration of simple enlightenment, it's very important to embrace that sweet body of yours. Let's take a little meditation break here and just allow our awareness to explore our physical self. You can access all the meditations online through sunimoon.net/readers.

Sit or lie down in a quiet place where you won't be interrupted. Let your eyes close if you can. If not, then just let your gaze softly rest on the wall or ceiling.

Take a nice, full breath in, and let the exhale air flow back out. Let your thoughts rest on your breath for a minute. Remember to watch if the mind wanders. When it does, note what it wandered to, then gently call it back to this moment, to the breathing or to the sensation of your body on your seat or your back on the floor.

Breathe in and out, slowing down, staying in this moment as you can. Bring your awareness to your head. Honestly, this is where our awareness is commonly focused. We almost seem like disembodied heads, floating through life. Scan over your head, face and neck and notice any place that is uncomfortable or tight. On your next inhale, imagine you are breathing in and sending this fresh energy to that uncomfortable area.

Let your attention drift down to shoulders and arms. Stay relaxed and imagine how you can move shoulders and arms. If moving them now feels right, do that. You could open arms wide, stretching your chest, or wrap them around you in a hug and stretch out your back. You could flap these arms like great wings. There are many movements and abilities related to arms and shoulders. Relax and scan over this area of your body and notice any discomfort or tightness. On your next inhale, breathe into this area of your body with special attention on any uncomfortable areas. On the exhale, imagine releasing any tension. Allow your attention to wander into the chest, the heart center. Imagine or visualize that you can breathe right into the heart center through the chest wall. Fresh air and life force energy fill your chest and torso. Keep breathing at your own pace and explore this sensation.

Float your attention down to your abdomen and hips. This area of the body is home to vital organs and great power in musculature. These powerful abdominal muscles help you stand tall and squat down low. Food is taken in and then passed through this part of our body. If you want to, allow your hands to rub your belly in a clockwise pattern, or however feels good.

Bring awareness to the backside of your body, in contact with the chair, floor, bed, or ground. This connection, even to your bed, is an energetic connection to Mother Earth. On your next exhale, imagine you can release any heavy energy, any denser thoughts or worries out through the back, down through the floor, down into the foundation of your building and deep into the earth. Our earth can take these energies and refine them to be used elsewhere. You're not dumping your junk, you're giving her energies that are rich and can be used in other ways.

Move your attention down to your legs, knees, ankles, and feet. There is so much power and energy here. Your strong limbs can get you where you want to go. However, they operate now, the original power and purpose is there- to help you stand tall, move forward and find your grounding to the earth. Let your attention move all the way down to the toes. Wiggle them and on your next exhale, send love and energy to this furthest location on the body from the head, heart, and lungs. Be thankful for your toes.

On the next inhale, shift your awareness to your whole body. This amazing creature is not a machine but animal- alive, breathing, and well. Remember to care for your body at least as well as you might care for your family dog with healthy food, fresh air, movement, light, and touch. On your next inhale, imagine you are allowing life force energy that flows in with the breath to move throughout your entire body, bringing healing and health to all aspects of you. You can love your body, just as it is. It is home to you and your mind, your emotions and your spirit. It has a beauty and power that isn't defined by photos in the media but as a vital part of your human existence. Remember to touch your body, appreciate your body, even talk kindly to it. Nourish it well and may it carry you safely for years to many wonderful experiences.

We get very busy in our lives with thoughts and responsibilities to others, but we have a lifelong duty to care for ourselves in this life- body, mind, emotions and spirit. Make time for you. No one else can care for you or know what you need in the present moment. Meditation time isn't just for the mind but also for you to check in and care for all aspects of the self- listening, caring, energizing, releasing.

How does connecting to your body help you?

Relating kindly to our bodies is a part of our learning to live as whole, complete beings. You're not a brain being carried thru life by a vehicle. Our bodies are our physical home and visual identification in this world. The body is also an important part of sensing, giving, receiving, offering comfort to yourself and to others. You are a living, breathing animal with an amazing body that is under your care. Connect with it. Love it.

How does connecting to your body help the world?

I hope that embracing your whole self- body, mind, emotions and energy helps you realize not only the power you have, but also the connection to others. We are so much more the same than we are different. Wanting to feed, clothe and shelter ourselves and those we love is a universal need- humans, animals, plants, and all. Connect to your body, then connect to the world full of bodies. You are here to serve a community. Embrace your body. Embrace the beauty of all bodies.

17

What is light

"Light is the only reality" -The Tibetan Book of the Dead

The word light is so important to me. I regularly say, "I send you light and love." I know often people don't really know what I mean. But as we move into this new world, a better understanding of that little word becomes important.

> *light- noun*
> *1. something that makes things visible or affords illumination*
> *2. Physics- also called luminous energy, radiant energy, electromagnetic radiation to which the organs of sight react*
> *3. a similar form of radiant energy that does not affect the retina, ultraviolet or infrared rays*
> *4. As a verb- to light means to kindle, to begin, to create, to ignite*

Light is the energy of illumination. Light can allow us to see, but light also applies to the energy of understanding and clarity. Saying that someone has "seen the light" doesn't mean they have found a lightbulb. It means they comprehend. Their mind, senses, spirit are illuminated. Light raises our vibration so we might see more, understand more, receive more, love more. Light comes from the sun, from man-made sources, but also comes from the human body- the heart and brain.

Light of science

Light is a form of electromagnetic radiation. In some wavelengths, we can see it with our eyes, but other wavelengths are not visible. Light fascinated renown physicist Albert Einstein. Einstein believed light was a particle (photon) and the flow of photons was a wave. Einstein is credited with saying, "As the area of light expands, so does the perimeter of darkness." In a sense, light pushes back the darkness. It appears that what he really said is, "as our circle of knowledge expands, so does the circumference of darkness surrounding it."[20] To me, this means by expanding our awareness, we just expose our ignorance. The more we come to know, the more we realize we do not know. Therefore, we see the space to learn more and are encouraged to grow.

Light in religion

Light is a cross-cultural symbol for knowledge, truth and awareness that takes on even deeper meanings when we look at its use in religious texts and traditions. Light references appear in many religious traditions from ceremonial usage to the symbolic presence of "divine light." We often hear references to light in religion as a "guiding light" for those who have lost their way to follow. Light calls to mind images of angels, halos and rays of light- all symbols of the divine.[21]

Light is referred to often in the Abrahamic religions and extends into broader, philosophical, and spiritual beliefs. Enlightenment is commonly related to Buddhist traditions, but the Age of Enlightenment in history was decidedly more philosophical, inspiring the individual to become free from religious rules.

In the Bible, the term light is a symbol of God's presence or sacredness. Hinduism uses light as the symbol of Brahman, the eternal essence or spirit of the universe. Hindus celebrate a festival of light, honoring the victory of good over evil. The Jewish tradition has a festival of light celebrating the survival of their people and the rededication of a historic temple. For Buddhists, light is a metaphor for understanding the truth, their goal of spiritual development. For some Lakota Sioux, a Native American tribe,, the south direction represents light and passage- the bringing life to earth and passage for souls out of this world. In Islam, Allah is the light of the heavens and earth, revealing truth in all things.

Light in metaphysics

There are many people who can see the light of an energy field around living beings. These auras exist around humans, plants, animals and also crystals.

> *aura- noun*
> 1. *The distinctive atmosphere or quality that seems to surround and be generated by a person, thing, or place. "The ceremony retained an aura of mystery."*
> 2. *(in spiritualism and some forms of alternative medicine) a supposed emanation surrounding the body of a living creature and regarded as an essential part of the individual. "Emotional, mental, and spiritual levels form an energy field around the body known as the aura."*

While aura reading isn't my forte, I have seen them as a gentle glow around friends in soft lighting. To those who read auras, I am told the colors vary depending on how the person is feeling. Different colors denote distinct energies or emotions. Interesting!

You may now grasp that light has energetic meaning, religious presence, and a scientific basis. It may feel significant to you or not. If I try to explain what light means to me, I likely won't bring more clarity, but I feel like I owe it to you. For me, light is a bit of a mystery. And no, I won't give up there and leave you hanging, although this will wax a bit woo-woo. Take it or leave it as all things here.

Light is your connection to spirit and beyond. Light is energy. Light can be absorbed by the skin or breathed in with your next breath. Light is fuel for the spirit, energy of source. Light is your connection to higher wisdom, healing, peace. Light may be an aspect of spirit. Am I talking in a circle here? Perhaps. Light is the sweet energy of wisdom, purpose, power, and healing. It comes from the source of all things, however you might define that. Light can come to us in many ways- sun, insights, the breath, through intention and more.

Light comes in to us, but we also create it and send it out. Light particles and biophotons are emitted from your body. Dr. Fritz-Albert Popp, a past Professor of Biophysics and Director of the International Institute of Biophysics in Germany, did some very interesting research on light and the human body. Popp uncovered stunning insights into the body's "light-based" physiology. [22]

> *"We know today that man, essentially, is a being of light. And the modern science of photobiology ... is presently proving this. In terms of healing, the implications are immense. We now know, for example, that quanta of light can initiate, or arrest, cascade-like reactions in the cells, and that genetic cellular damage can be virtually repaired, within hours, by faint beams of light. We are still on the threshold of fully understanding the complex relationship between light and life, but we can now say emphatically, that the function of our entire metabolism in dependent on light." - Dr. Fritz-Albert Popp*[22]

Light is both a particle and a wave. Thank you, Dr. Einstein. A photon can travel indefinitely. There is no limit to its reach. It does not lose energy in travel. Therefore, if I send you light, it can reach you.

Light is my highest commodity, a combination of the physical and spiritual realm, carrying all the good energy that the recipient or the world might need. That definition leads me to believe that people are drawn to the light as moths to a flame. The specific definition may have a lot to do with what you seek and what you see as the power behind all things. Whatever you conclude, I still choose to say, I am sending you light and love.

I have tried to define something that I first told you is a bit of a mystery. What I think light is and does, will work for me. Explore what you think of this lovely energy. It is an amazing power to change your perspective and your life.

How working with light can help you?

Opening to the existence of light and its power- physical, emotional, spiritual, helps each of us not feel alone. You are not an island, scrambling for survival to find power and resources alone. There is a plan, there are resources. Beyond the physical… beyond the logical… there is light. Open to it.

How working with light helps the world?

Understanding that light is here to help us and to allow us to help others brings me great comfort. When my great nephew was born, he was in NICU for several weeks. I couldn't see him, but I could send him light. When we hear of strife in the world, we can send money, of course. But we can also send light to areas of the world fraught with conflict, disaster or need. I can visualize better times for all the people in the world. I can send light to fill them with hope. It is a real, measurable form of assistance, even if embracing this concept feels new to you.

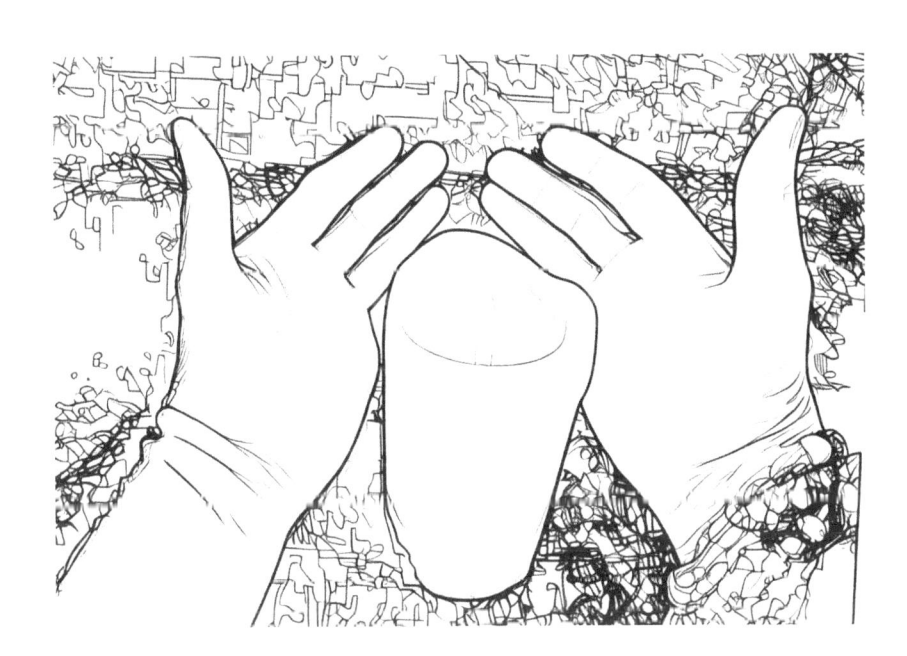

this journey

18

Your body's energy system

Energy- what is it, how can we work with it? Ah, here we go on another big explanation of a hard to grasp concept. Maybe it's better to say many people see or define this word differently? To me, when I speak of energy in the body, I'm referring to life force energy. I see energy as a power in the body to heal, to operate itself at its optimum and as a radiant energy affecting those around me and the world. There is an energy system in the human body, in case that is a new concept for you. As in all chapters here, I'm going to touch lightly on this vast and beautiful topic to give you some basic understanding so we might move forward in the book together. If you want more- oh my friend, there is a universe of information about energy and how you can work with it. For now, the basics.

Where does this healing, life force energy come from? We all are balls of energy. The earth, the sun, the ocean, the air, the cosmos- all composed of energy. The world is awash in energy. In our culture, the medical community doesn't acknowledge the energy system in the body, yet. I'm sure that's a part of the reason so many people don't know about or consider this energy as real or important. There is current research that is pointing to the fascia as being part of this energy system, but studies are ongoing. Remember that mantra I've been chanting to you- physical and spiritual, visible and invisible, practical/logical and magical? Yes, this healing energy is in the spiritual, invisible, magical realm. Personal energy is another aspect of life that was not important in the old world and will be so important in this new one.

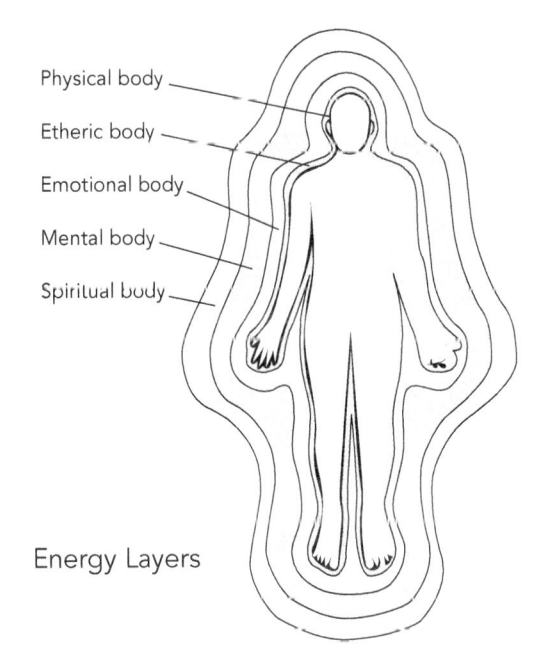

Physical body
Etheric body
Emotional body
Mental body
Spiritual body

Energy Layers

The idea of the body's energy system might seem new or even new age. But working with the energy system of life is only relatively new to westerners. Many ancient cultures understand and work with the energy meridians of the body. Many healing methods, such as Traditional Chinese Medicine, the Indian Ayurvedic tradition, and the Hindu chakra system, have recognized that the human body is primarily energy. For thousands of years, indigenous cultures have seen the human body as an energy system with the innate ability to heal itself. For ancient cultures, there was no division between body, mind and spirit; all worked together seamlessly. Plato wrote in 380 BCE in "The Republic" that physicians erred when they separated the soul from the body by providing healing and cures. [23]

While the terminology varies from culture to culture, the concept of working with the body's energy field is similar. In China, the energy is called *chi*. In Japan, it is *ki,* and in India the energy forces are known as *prana*. The Buddha talked about *virya*, meaning vitality or the energy of life. All these terms are describing the life force, the spark of life. Just as the circulatory system brings blood, and the lymphatic system carries off waste, the energy system brings life force energy to all areas of the body. As a blockage in the circulatory system causes disease and other consequences, similar problems occur when the energy system is blocked. Energy flows within the body and radiates around it as well, commonly called an aura.

For our purposes, I want to address energy in the body in general terms. For those interested in more details, there are layers of energy around the body and channels of energy that run through the body. There are energy centers. Depending on the tradition, the energy centers are called chakras, gates, belts, or wheels. You can find many resources for more info about the details by studying chakras, energy meridians, acupressure points or even reflexology. Have fun! For now, I want to focus more on the amount and the quality of the energy in and around your body in basic terms, and how you can navigate, work with and improve energetic conditions around you.

How to connect with your energy? Well, you already do that. It's common to feel as if your energy is low, you feel tired or sluggish. Energy too high leaves you feeling wired, anxious, or jittery. As you learn and work more with energy, you'll sometimes feel it as a tingling, warm, or buzzy feeling flowing through your body. Some feel it easily and some don't. Your energy is always coursing through your body as it is life. Energy levels can be adjusted by using simple practices to work with the body's energy.

Society suggests we can shift our energy and our emotional states by adjusting our body chemistry by adding more coffee, or a little wine, but we can also use the body's energy with no additional ingredients needed.

You might wonder, as this energy is invisible and magical, how can you work with it? Honestly, a lot of energy work is intention. But there are some practical/logical ways that create a physical experience of this seemingly esoteric medium. A simple exercise to play with energy is to rub the palms of your hands together briskly. You feel heat from friction, but that heat also shows that you've moved extra energy into your hands. Place your palms about 3 inches apart and focus on the sensations between your hands. Move them a little closer, then further, and notice how the sensations change. What some of you are feeling is the energy radiating from one hand to another. This is something that works better for some than others. It's also a practiced skill and is enhanced by intention. If you sit down to prove that this illusive healing life force energy isn't real, then you will often get the result you wish for.

You can move the energy in your body by moving your hands or by using intention, visualization, imagination, or pretending. Remember that we now live in a world of the practical/logical AND magical. I hope to help you get more familiar with the idea that what we envision or believe is activated in our body and in our world. Sometimes it helps to take yourself back to your child-self. A child believes in magic and is open to the awe and wonder of life. I have worked with healing energy for many years. It's true, powerful and available to all. Try approaching this energy play with that mindset.

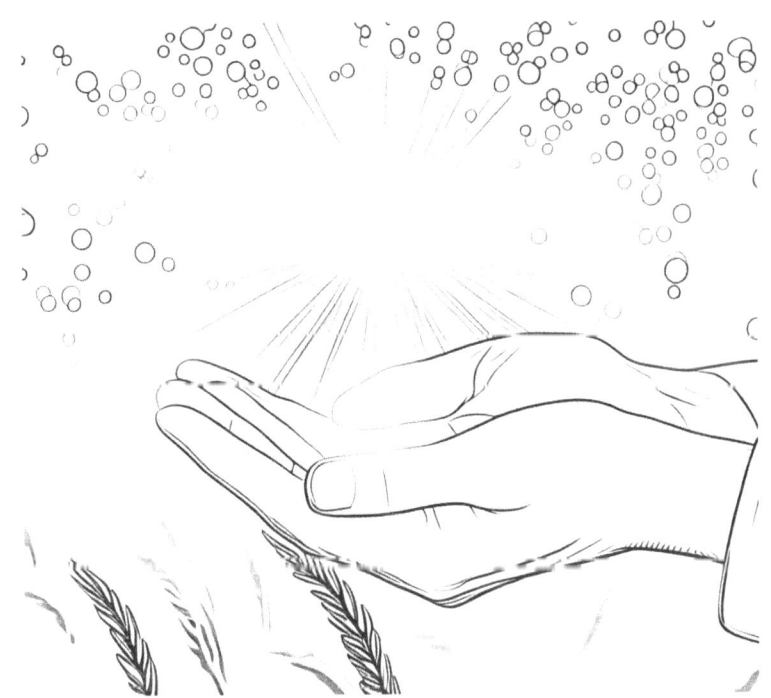

this *journey*

Energy comes in different types, with different purposes and results. There's calm energy, energy that enlivens you, energy that feels clear/clean and energy that feels busy or complicated. Let's pretend energy has a sound. Imagine one clear musical note being played on the piano. Someone is playing one note every few seconds, repeating the same note again and again. It's clear, clean and simple. These sounds I'll equate to calm energy, or clean energy. Now imagine that your 3-year-old has discovered the piano and is banging away on many keys at once. Many notes, many rhythms, not necessarily harmonious. This is still sound or music, but this situation creates a very different feeling in the listener. I would consider this energy as dense or complicated. This kind of energy can feel like it's distracting us or weighing us down.

We pull pure, clear energy into our body in many ways. You can breathe it in with the air. Feel it shining down from the sun. Receive energy through the skin, through our eyes and through the energy centers in the body- primarily the root center or chakra at the base of the spine, the heart center and the crown chakra at the top of the head. We can receive energy directly from the earth by lying on it, or digging our bare feet into the soil. We can pull energy in through connection and intention. There is a wealth of energy available to us and many ways to receive it, so the challenge is just to be aware of energy as a factor in your health and wellness.

I studied recently with the Q'ero people in the high mountains of Peru. Their teachings are beautiful, simple and very earth based. One tenet was repeated again and again, "There is no bad energy." Just as they believe there are no bad people, no bad weather. Some things might be more challenging, more complicated, offer more lessons, but not bad. So no bad energy, just dense energy.

I'd like to lead you in a meditation or visualization of receiving, moving, and exchanging energy. Try to find a time when you won't be disturbed. Realize that in most locations, there will be some outside noise, so just tell yourself that you will not allow outside noise to distract you from your visualization, unless the noise is something that truly requires your attention.

more Find this meditation and other resources online at SuniMoon.net/readers

Sit or lie down in a quiet place. Let your eyes close if you can. If not, then just gaze softly at the wall or ceiling.

Take a nice, full breath in, and exhale air back out. Let your thoughts rest on your breath for a minute or so. Remember to watch if the mind wanders. When it does, note what it wandered to, then gently call it back to this moment, to the breathing or to the sensation of your body on your seat or your back on the floor.

Breathe in and out, slowing down, staying in this moment as you can.

When you inhale, you are receiving oxygen, but you're also pulling in energy, life force energy. This isn't a conscious effort, it's just one natural way your body receives energy. When you exhale, the used gases flow out, but the energy stays with you.

On the exhale, allow yourself to release a bit of tension, stress, or pain. You receive on the inhale and release on the exhale. In and out. Receive and release. Stay with that for a minute or more.

Imagine, pretend or visualize that the energy first fills your chest, then flows or floats on through your body, filling the torso, then flowing out to fingers and toes, up to your head. This isn't forced, just a gentle floating motion, perhaps a bit like watching a leaf float down a gentle creek.

Allow your attention to scan through your body, seeking areas that are weak or painful. On your next inhale, imagine you are directing some of this energy to those areas of your body that need support. Again, stay loose and in the moment, just letting energy flow on your inhale, then imagine releasing a bit of your tension, stress or pain on the exhale. Keep scanning and send energy to areas of your body that need support.

Breath at your own pace, continue breathing and using the energy you receive as you need it. Release stress, tension, pain, worries, and other dense, complicated energies on your exhale. Allow your awareness to drift throughout your body with gratitude and appreciation for all it does for you.

How working with energy helps you?

Working with my energy system gives me another tool to connect all the aspects of me. Flowing energy from the soles of my feet to the top of my head reminds me of the reach and power of my physical self. Visualizing the energy surrounding me seems to make my spiritual, emotional and mental self more accessible somehow. Explore and see how working with energy might help you.

How working with energy helps the world?

I like to remember that there is no bad energy. There is dense or complicated energy. I can send clear, clean energy to another person or another part of the world and that can be helpful to another. It's also a reminder of our connection. All energy, available to all, all connected.

19

Using energy in healing

I hope you all have experienced, either as the giver or the receiver, the comfort that comes when a someone kisses away a child's pain from a skinned knee. Our care givers have offered comfort to children and loved ones for all the ages. This instinct to offer comfort is the simplest way of using energy as a healer. Holding, rocking, and kissing the hurt or pain of another person is known as magnetic healing, where you give your energy for another's well being. However, as you repeatedly give healing this way, your energy level can be lowered.

In magnetic healing, you, as the healer, are the source of the healing energy. This works beautifully with a child with a skinned knee from time to time. Living in our transformed world, we often face things we wish to change. Your energy is a real way to offer help in many situations. Helping others regularly with your own energy can quickly exhaust you. You alone are not an inexhaustible source of energy, yet you live in a world that is.

How much energy is available to you to help the world? In my experience, we are receiving energy from a universal source, and it is unlimited. I always have what I need to help another as it's not my power, my knowledge that's helping them. The energy of love, of light, of spirit, is what is doing the work. Helping another in this way shouldn't deplete you. I am often energized just from flowing fresh energy through my client and myself.

The key here is that you are not doing the work. You might choose to help, to heal, to lift, to change, but it's not you acting alone on your own power that brings good. Realize your connection to something larger, some source of power of goodness, or healing, or peace is supplying the energy. This is an important step in our growing from that adolescent being, the I/me/mine mindset, to seeing us all as connected and interdependent. Thich Nhat Hanh uses a term "interbeing" that feels quite nice to me.

this *journey*

Interbeing conveys the concept that all things interconnected, a state of being related and interdependent. The energy we pull in to do our work, play, healing is the same energy available to all. The energy is of peace, love, and compassion.

> *"Interbeing is the understanding that nothing exists separately from anything else. We are all interconnected. By taking care of another person, you take care of yourself. By taking care of yourself, you take care of the other person. Happiness and safety are not individual matters. If you suffer, I suffer. If you are not safe, I am not safe. There is no way for me to be truly happy if you are suffering. If you can smile, I can smile too. The understanding of interbeing is very important. It helps us to remove the illusion of loneliness, and transform the anger that comes from the feeling of separation." -Thich Nhat Hanh, How to Fight*[2]

Now, let's shift from "how I can help myself" with my knowledge of life force energy to a role of "how can I help the world" with this energy? We can bring in fresh energy for our own energy field and to share. There are many ways to bring in energy. Get outside when the sun is shining. Allow the morning sun to shine on your face and imagine pulling energy in through the top of your head or through your eyes without, of course, looking directly at the sun. I gaze at the light glittering on the trees in the morning dew. Stand on the earth and breathe energy up through your feet. Even if you can't be outdoors, visualize connecting to the earth and the sky, both sources of energy to you. We can truly breathe in the energy any time we need it. Let's start there.

When you're beginning to study the body's energy, it's easiest to start with pulling in energy through the breath. Breathing brings in energy along with oxygen, increasing your life force energy and vitality. Remember your breath anytime you're feeling depleted, nervous or anxious. It is an amazing calming and empowering tool. Try breathing with me.

> *Begin by increasing your awareness of how your breath is naturally flowing. Notice where the body moves as you breathe and listen to the sound of your inhalation and exhalation. After a few breaths, begin to deepen and expand the breath and make sure you are breathing through your nose if you can. As you inhale, draw the breath into the belly. Allow the abdomen to expand with the breath. Continue this inhalation, expanding through the rib cage and upper chest.*

It may be helpful to place one hand on your belly and the other on your chest to feel the expansion as you inhale. Take as much time as you need to get a full, deep breath, but don't force the breath. Then allow that breath to flow back out, slowly and evenly through the nose or mouth. Repeat and notice how you feel. Notice rib expansion on front, sides and back. Feel a bit of expansion in the upper chest at the end of your inhalation. We're all different. Explore what feels good to you. This may change as you practice more.

Breathing is an incredibly powerful place to build new habits. I have been taught that 70% of the toxins in the body can be expelled in the breath. The teacher that shared this with me challenged us to take 5 deep breaths several times a day. Conscious breathing might become your practice first thing in the morning, as a break at work or on the drive home. Deep breathing, not hyper-ventilation, but deep, slow belly breathing, can help our body in so many ways.

Practice this deeper, slower breathing for a minute or so and notice if it changes how you feel. If I'm feeling depleted, this style of breathing energizes me. If I need to calm, this same breath can also calm me. Breathing is my number one tool to bring in more energy for myself and to work with others. Breathing is there for us any time. When stressed, our breathing naturally becomes more shallow and rapid to force higher oxygen levels into the blood. This allows explosive action. After the danger that brought the fight-or-flight response is passed, then breathing can return to a deeper, relaxed pace.

What other ways to attract and draw in the energy to share with others?

I begin where I begin all new things, with imagination and visualization. What follows is a meditation to pull in light. Read through it, then personalize it. When you're doing these sorts of meditations alone, you don't need to read the words, you can just tell a story in your mind. If your mind wanders too much, you can play the online recording. Visualization, imagination, or meditation put you into a deep state of relaxation, so it is not appropriate to play meditation recordings while at work or driving. As with all the meditations in this book, the online version is at SuniMoon.net/readers

this journey

To experience a meditation or visualization, put yourself in a comfortable position sitting or lying down. Try to find a time when you might not be interrupted. Realize that often there will be outside noise. Tell yourself that you will not allow outside noise to distract you from your visualization, unless the noise is something that truly requires your attention.

Sit or lie in a comfortable position. Allow your eyes to close and take a deep breath. Release this breath naturally, then just observe your breathing. Think about breathing in all the way to your abdomen, so it inflates a bit as you inhale. This is the breathing of an infant, if you've ever watched one. Slow, deeper breathing is very healthy breathing for anyone, as it uses more of your lung capacity. So relax and breathe into your belly, then let the chest expand and when you're ready, exhale slowly. Allow your body to settle into a comfortable position. Give yourself time to relax into this breathing, long and slow as feels comfortable.

Continue breathing but imagine with every breath in, you are bringing in oxygen, energy and light. The connection between energy and light is common, so imagine you are breathing in bright white light (or some other color as feels right to you.) With every inhale, more air, energy and light. As you exhale, the spent air is released, but the energy and light remain inside.

Visualize, imagine, or pretend that first just your lungs light up. As you continue breathing, your arms, your whole torso, your legs become gradually filled with light. Your fingers, toes, your head, your eyes, all filled with this beautiful, bright light. If we turned the lights down in the room, you could see the light shining out of the pores in your skin. So much light that it fills the space around your body. First just a few inches outside your skin, and with a few more breaths, you are sitting in a big light-emitting egg.

On your next breath, reach your arms out, hands open, fingers spread wide and scoop a huge armload of this light. Sweep your hands to your chest, bringing more light right into your heart center. Hold your hands over your heart, sealing this moment while releasing all the rest of the light to the world, to help, lift, awaken and make peace. Realize that this energy is available to you at any moment, to help you and to help the world. Any time you need it, the energy is there to lift and fill you so that you can share with another person, near or far away. Relax, breathe and enjoy the peacefulness, the lack of need that this energy can bring. Rest, breathe and enjoy.

This work with energy can go further. You can pull in energy, fill your reservoirs, then send it to others. Yes, share energy through your intention, your imagination, your visualization. Many are quite comfortable with the concept of prayer, asking some far off spiritual entity to send their energy or magic to a person or place in need. In working with healing energy, we're just realizing that the spiritual connection is within us. The mystic power and wisdom that was moved far away from us was never truly gone. Pull in energy and send it out to our hurting world, to help open eyes and hearts to ways to bring more love and compassion for all.

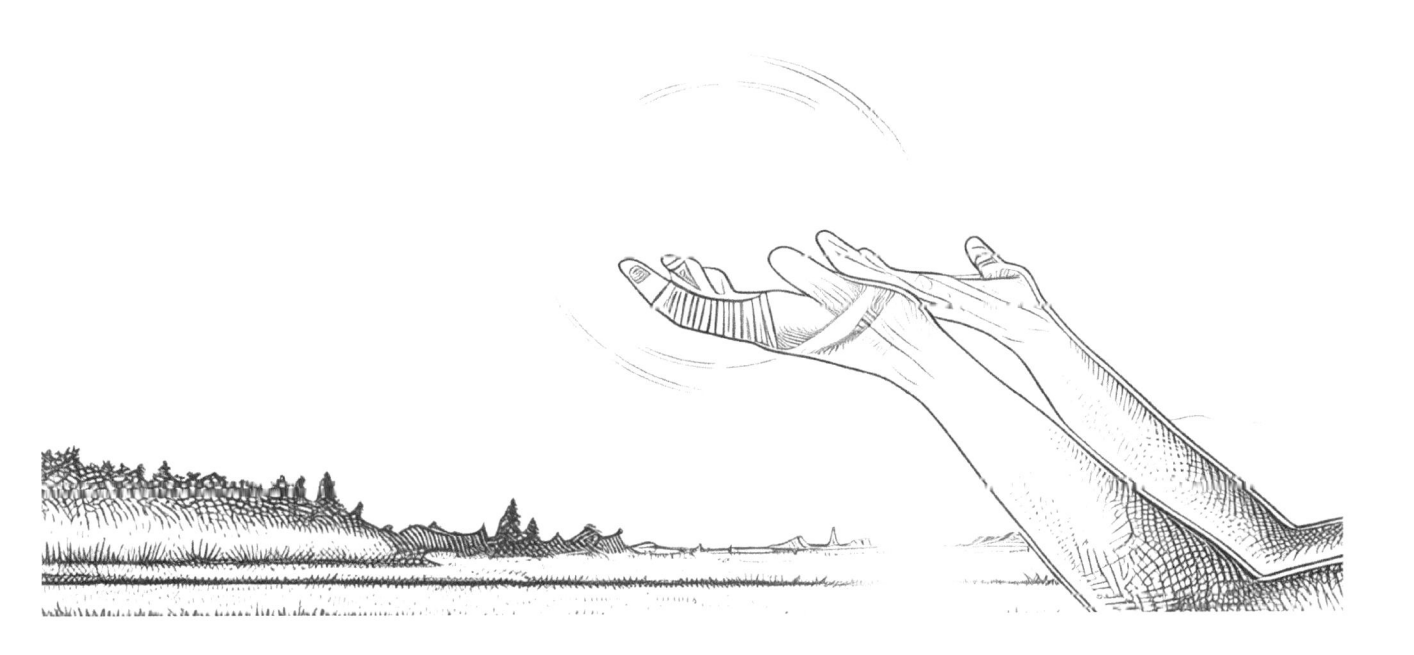

How does using the body's energy in healing help you?

For me, understanding the energy system gives me one more tool to help- myself and others. We have been so trained that if we don't feel good, step 1 is to go see a doctor or a therapist. I'm not saying those are wrong choices, but you also can add this power of helping yourself to the options. You can empower your body's energy system to help build wellness. If you are ill, following the plan from your medical professional can be supplemented by also using energy to help your body heal.

How does using the body's energy in healing help the world?

The body's energy system isn't contained within the skin. It exists inside and outside your physical body. It might be the first way you actually connect with another. To me, my energy is part of the same energy source as your energy. I can't call in energy for me without surrounding you with its goodness as well. It is another part of our global, cosmic community, our connection to all things. You can offer help to all in this way.

Intention and visualization

Our thoughts are another powerful energy source. Did you know that your body physiology responds to your thoughts as though they are real? Yes, something doesn't actually have to be happening. You might just be conjuring or worrying, and the body reacts as though what you imagined is happening right here and now. You know this is true. Let's think about a peach (or substitute some favorite treat of yours if you're not a peach fan.) Visualize peaches in summer, freshly picked from a tree, still warm from the sun. Imagine you're walking through your favorite farmers' market on a quest for fresh peaches.

You see the stand ahead, organic fresh peaches sitting in a basket calling to you. You reach out and pick one up, in its soft furry little jacket. You bite into it (of course, with the shopkeeper's permission and assurance that she washed it well for you) and the flavor just explodes in your mouth. That sweet, fresh peach smells and tastes perfect. The juice is dripping down your chin. Ahhh. Now, peach lover, are you salivating? Just the thought of a favorite food elicits salivation. So just imagining the peach brought a physical reaction.

My point is your thoughts are powerful as a manifestation tool. How can we harness that power to work in our favor? We can by exploring intention and visualization. First, what is an intention?

> intention noun
> 1. a thing intended; an aim or plan. "she was full of good intentions"
> 2. MEDICINE- the healing process of a wound

Our intentions are our plans, our dreams. They're not resolutions, things we have to fix, solving shortcomings. An intention is more a guide, a direction towards more of whatever you are seeking in this life. Intention is us becoming more- healing, growing, reaching towards our true self. An intention

this journey

is a way to aim towards a better future. An intention can set you in motion on the path of purpose. I love that in the definition above, intention is also explained as a medicine, a part of healing.

visualization, noun
1. *the representation of an object, situation, or set of information as a chart or other image.* "video systems allow visualization of the entire gastrointestinal tract,"
2. *chart or other image that is created as a visual representation of an object, situation or information.*
3. *the formation of a mental image of something.*

We imagined the peach and found that visualizing clearly with all our senses involved, brings about a change in our bodies, a change in the physical realm. In the same way, visualization can empower our plans, our dreams, our purpose.

Positive affirmations can be a powerful tool for some. But for many, they don't work at all. Why? Because the affirmer doesn't believe in the affirmation's truth. My lips might say "I love and honor myself" but the mind could be saying "I'm not a good person, I'm not worthy of love and honor." When this sort of thing happens, we are actually affirming the negative, because our emotions believe the affirmation is not true.

If you've been reading this book from the start, then you have begun the journey to seeing that you are an amazing being of physical and spiritual wonder. However, buried in your sub-conscious may be old habits/labels of seeing yourself in a negative light. Intentions and visualizations are perfect tools to help us reprogram old habitual thoughts. We can use these two tools together to help change beliefs held in our subconscious. To begin with intention and visualization, break out your pen and journal. Start with jotting down ideas some aspects of you that you wish to empower. Working on intentions is a creative process. We explore, then adjust, rewrite, and redefine. Writing your intentions in a journal allows you to look back in the future, assess progress, and congratulate yourself on how far you have come.

"You get what you intend to create by being in harmony with the power of intention, which is responsible for all of creation." -Dr. Wayne Dyer [24]

The healing aspect of intention is important. When we think about our personal trauma, our first reaction might be to consider how we got hurt or who caused it. If you still carry deep pain from some wound in your life, I suggest you spend some time with a good therapist to help you find peace with that. I've put in good healing time with therapists during my life and have found them to be very helpful, especially with deep trauma that's too big for me to understand how to handle.

As you begin to explore areas you'd like to heal, remember to be an objective observer as we recall events that might have wounded us. We don't have to bleed again. That wound is healed. Acknowledge the thing that hurt us long ago. We learned from that experience, grew stronger, and we survived. Now we intend to bring more healing and empower ourselves to grow past any limitation we still carry. We can visualize ourselves being stronger and wiser for those experiences. We leave our history in the past, believe in our strength and thrive in the now.

Let's imagine I want to build an intention that will help me become a more physically healthy being, to move my body with grace and freedom. This is a lovely, positive vision. To increase movement in my life means I have to make some time in my schedule for myself. I must value myself more. I will care for myself with the same love and importance as I do for my children or my partner. Perhaps my movement is best done outdoors, so my intention might include exploring nature more. Taking the time to get outdoors to absorb the great peace and wisdom from a forest is about more than just moving. This intention might have grown into, "I will schedule self-care into my day as one of my highest priorities because it affects my health, happiness and longevity."

Can you see how these intentions can be more effective than deciding you need 15 minutes of calisthenics in the morning? See how they reach further and can make this goal really important in how it affects all of your life? Visualize this intention changing your life, how it can make you feel, and how it helps you better fulfill your purpose.

Some pointers about writing intentions

1. Keep your statement in the positive. For example "I am giving my self-care as high a priority as I do caring for others." Not "I will not neglect self-care."

Our minds are funny things. Some wise teacher taught me to imagine the word "not" as being incomprehensible by my mind. If I were to say, "I will not neglect self-care," my mind will have a tendency to grab onto "neglect self-care." You might not agree with this concept, but it has served me well and can help train us to think in the positive. Another hint- no words like "try", "but", "except" in an intention. Write as if your intention is happening now. "I give my self-care the highest priority." "I make time to enjoy nature and get some fresh air." Writing in the now is also a sort of mind game. If I say, "I will…" do something, my mind can say, "I will… sometime, but not right now. I'm too busy."

2. Include feelings in your intentions. Think about what you'll be gaining by making the changes you're considering. Our intention isn't just for the body but for the mind, emotions, and spirit. For example, "I give my self-care the highest priority for increased health and increased feelings of power and vitality."

3. Make your intention focus on end results. For example, I wish for more physical health and strength in life. I could resolve to do 30 minutes of exercise in the morning and take a run at lunchtime. Specifics like this reek of resolutions to me. Some days, these conditions don't work out. You are intending what to do at the start without visualizing the end goal and results. Visualize life when your feelings of health and strength have grown. What do you look and feel like? Picture yourself doing things that are a challenge now. Imagine you have accomplished this intention.

Have you gotten your intention written so it feels effective to you? Now what? I used to write intentions once a year around the Winter Solstice time. Then near the Summer Solstice I'd read them again. Often I'd find I hadn't made progress. I had made the Solstice my report card time, and I wasn't getting very good grades.

Intention and visualization

Enter visualization. Your old habits/beliefs have been ingrained in your mind, in your subconscious, by years of repetition. That means that to make a new intention effective, we need to do the same, with repetition. Put your intentions somewhere you will see them. Maybe taped on the bathroom mirror so you can review your intentions while brushing your teeth? I have an intentions page in my journal that is bookmarked. I open to it every morning and read those intentions first.

Rote reading of intentions, then dashing off to your day will not help you. Pause and read the intention. Remember why this change is important. Reflect on how you will feel once you have achieved this change. Really feel those feelings. "My body moving confidently and without pain" might feel empowering or freeing. Honor this intention. Visualize living life when this change has become your norm, your habit. We have to engage our emotions in this process to expedite change. Visualization, like thinking about that fresh peach, brings response from our body, mind and spirit.

Visualization is a tool you can use to teach yourself something new. The body, mind, emotions, and spirit connect and respond to what you are thinking. Visualization is a multi-sensory experience. We're not just reading black words of our intention written on a white page. We read words and then pause, actively picturing in our mind's eye how it will look, feel, and smell when our intention is fulfilled. Feel the smile on your face. Feel your heart full and satisfied. Feel the joy and love radiating all around you. Visualization is the key to empowering our intentions. How you do it is your call. I read my intentions, then fold my hands over my heart center, often lying back in bed, and I pretend, imagine, visualize me and my world when this intention has born fruit in my life. I feel the warmth, the peace, the assuredness of accomplishment. I see the joy, the support that my intention can bring to me, to others and to our world. Then I get up and take action to make the intentions reality.

> "Your imagination allows you the fabulous luxury of thinking from the end. There's no stopping anyone who can think from the end." -Dr. Wayne Dyer, The Power of Intention[24]

You are seeing positive results in your mind's eye, the end results of your fulfilled intention. You play that "happy ending" in the movie of your intention. Then your body, mind and spirit and your universal connection to all as you understand it, can manifest the power you need to make that intention come true. You aren't in this alone. You have all the power of the universe supporting you.

How long does it take? Good question. I've often read that it takes 21 or 24 days to make a new habit. However, recently I read some research that places the number more at 66 days.[25] For me, it takes a long time, meaning I keep repeating the intentions even when they're being fulfilled just so I don't slide back into an old, lifelong habit. You navigate this however you feel will work for you.

How do intention and visualization help you?

Both these practices require that I focus on the positive. I am setting goals, plans, a path towards what I want, while letting go of what I don't want. I am challenged to repeat these positive images/visions often. I am training my brain. I am forming new habits. These skills can carry over into all areas of my life. Watch and see.

How do intention and visualization help the world?

Just as we can practice seeing ourselves as healed, joyful and accomplished, we can use intention and visualization to build a loving and compassionate world. Consider turning off the news and spending 10 minutes setting intentions and visualizing this new world and your role in it. You can empower yourself and your positive visions and energy can empower others.

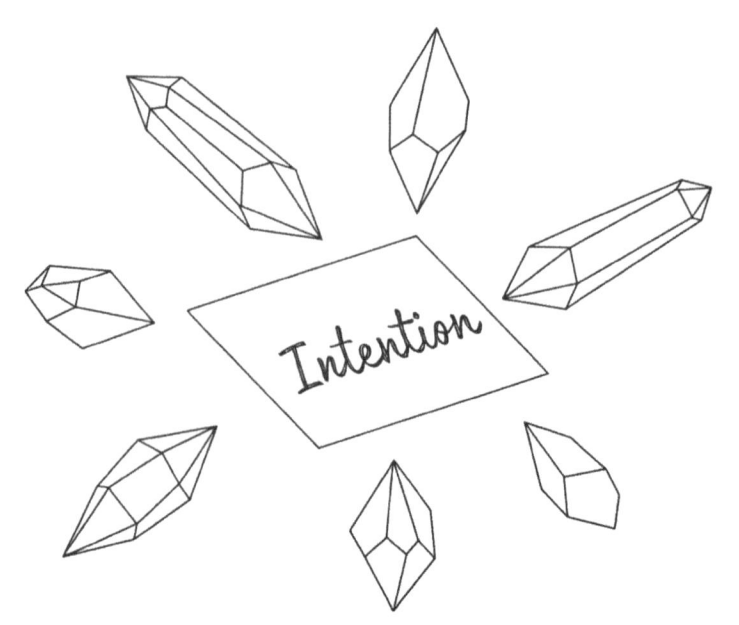

21

Your inner wisdom is infallible

Many of us learned growing up that god was somewhere far away. He had rules. He needed our money, and you had to please him. When society separated humans from the divine, life shifted. No longer was holiness all around you, in plants, in the earth, the sun, the stars… it was somewhere else. Why this shift? Perhaps to keep the masses more manageable as the agricultural and industrial revolutions took place. Food and shelter were no longer a part of life. You had to earn your place in modern society. Religions often put a barrier between humans and the divine. You needed to see a priest, pastor, rabbi, mullah, imam to learn about god or to reach the divine. You need a mediator to connect with holiness. That is a significant lie to me. You don't need anyone to connect to the divine, to holiness, because you are the divine. Whatever you see as god, source, goddess, universal consciousness, _____… your connection to that is within. That hotline to highest wisdom is a part of who you are. It always has been.

When the spiritual you jumped on board with your physical body, your unbreakable link to the divine/spirit/energy was made. Call your spiritual aspect what you wish- spirit, soul, higher self, the superconscious. I'm talking about the essence of you, the invisible you, the part that goes on after the body falls apart. I like to think of this aspect of me as my inner wisdom. When we practiced being the observer in meditation, who do you think the observer was? I think my observer, the one that can watch my busy brain spin around in circles and not get sucked in, is my higher self, my inner wisdom. You can connect with your higher self with no shaman or holy person. You slide right into that inner wisdom because it's always been there in you. You can use it, but perhaps weren't taught or encouraged about its power.

This inner wisdom is your spiritual aspect. It is a divine, essential part of the universal consciousness. Many believe that when your body dies, this aspect of you returns to being a part of the source of all things, while still maintaining a bit of your individuality. But your connection to source, to god is there while your body is alive and well. Some of us think of inner wisdom as our intuition… "I don't know where that idea came from, but it's great!" It came from the higher, wiser you.

I don't want to try to define the undefinable here, but hope to share the concept that the higher you is onboard, Your enlightened self is not floating out in the galaxy waiting for you to get your shit together. Awakening is embracing the fact that there is a higher, wiser, spiritual you within. It is part of the great unknown, the source, the god, therefore your higher self is amazingly wise.

I remember many years ago when I was trying to find my place in the Christian church; I was having a discussion with a teacher. I shared my "translation" of a Bible passage and he explained that my sense of the meaning was wrong. I said something to the effect that, "if the Holy Spirit of God is dwelling in me, I have a hotline to the big guy himself in my heart. How can my heart-felt interpretation of these words be wrong?" I was told that in time, I'd learn to respect and follow the church leaders in these matters. We all would agree on interpretations. Yeah, well, as you might guess, I didn't fit there. (smirk) While my younger self's discussion with the church elder wasn't very respectful or graceful, I still believe it was right. We have knowledge within us, knowledge we do not know how it got there. Some think of this inner knowledge as intuition or psychic ability, but to me, this inner wisdom is my divine self and, as such, it is infallible.

Using such a forceful word as infallible makes people uncomfortable. I know. Am I saying that I know it all? Well, yes, in a way. My inner wisdom, my higher self, my spirit, knows exactly what I should do. Notice the pronoun there. I know what _I should do_. I don't know what you should do. Each of us has a sweet, unique path to our purpose here on earth. I believe that my spiritual guidance is perfect for me. I know (or have a pretty good idea) what my next step should be. I don't know what my 99th step should be. I am confident after many years of following this belief, that my spirit will never lead me wrong.

When I ignore my inner hunches, my gut instincts, sometimes things go to hell. Making wrong choices is part of a life-long learning experience. Once you've chosen wrong a few thousand times, you gain a greater respect for that tiny, wise voice within. Do I always seek higher wisdom today? Most of the time, yes. Sometimes I still have to stick my finger in the light socket, so to speak. That's part of being physical and spiritual to me. Both aspects of me are still learning how to be more when they work together.

I did say that my higher wisdom never leads me wrong. Yes, never. Now remember, we are talking about our higher selves. I have to be still, breathe, calm myself, and seek my spiritual guidance. I am not excluding my brain's input from my insights and decisions. As I've been saying throughout the book, the trick is to merge our physical and spiritual, our onboard computer with our direct connection to higher wisdom. Put those two parts together and magic can happen. When approached with care and calm, I always know what to do. Yes, when I follow the leading of higher wisdom along with the support of my calm mind, I've never been led wrong. However, when I follow my higher direction, a day or so later, I might get new insights.

It's like setting out on a hike. I decide at the beginning which trail to follow. Then I hike awhile, to the top of the hill, and oh, what a view. At that place, because I have a new perspective, new info and I might adjust my path. Inner wisdom works that way. The key is to pause, connect, and listen. Take some time and ponder what the message is. Meditate on the same question again later. But at some point, it's crucial that you and I trust and set out on the hike. We must begin or we miss the chance for new perspectives and additional information.

Practicing communication with your higher self is just that- a practice. You get better and better at it. The connection becomes easier with experience. In time, you can develop a sense of security in knowing that you have a source of great wisdom for you and your path in life.

Our higher wisdom deals in a world of love and compassion. If you ever unsure about a choice, choose the more loving option. Higher wisdom won't guide us to resort to the actions of the old world. It won't direct you to hurt, damage, steal, lie, or create fear. Higher wisdom is here to help us elevate the new world of love and compassion. We're not talking about getting our way, or getting more money, power, or stuff. We're truly trying to make the world a better, more loving and compassionate place.

We are living in a time of amazing change. I don't have to worry about who's going to fix this mess, or who is going to save us. All I have to do is get still, listen and I hear direction for what I should do to make the best of the day ahead of me. This inner wisdom takes the fear away in time. We don't have to listen to the news or decide which guru to follow. We have our guru onboard. We always have.

How does reliance on inner wisdom help you?

Other people love to tell you what they think you should do. Often their intentions are good. However, no one knows what you should do. Others only know what they would do in what they perceive as your circumstances. They may truly want the best for you, but no one knows your deep life lessons and purpose. I don't avoid listening to the suggestions of others. They might share information that can help me find my way. But the ultimate truth for me always comes from deep within my heart/gut… from my higher self.

How does reliance on inner wisdom help the world?

I suppose I could just take the paragraph above and switch the pronouns around. How often do you catch yourself saying, "You know what you should do?" Yeah, stop that, please. Offering a kind suggestion to another if they've asked your opinion is perfectly fine. Remember, you only know what you would do in their situation as you perceive it. You don't deeply know their purpose, strengths, or life experience.

As we embrace our role as serving our global, cosmic community, we as a circle or group might be called to set a direction for our community. Remember… open your heart, search your gut and don't lead with your busy brain's input. Proceed with great gentleness, love and compassion in planning how this new world will blossom.

22

Teach from within

As we grow into our fully human selves (body, mind, emotions, and spirit), a sense of purpose is often clear. Dreams about ways to help others. Do we form an organization to do ____? Could we teach about ____? Whatever loving ideas come to you, they are excellent. Now, how to begin? Do you wonder if you're really ready?

How do you become ready to teach a skill or interest that is important or even a passion of yours? Well, in this country, we sign up for more schooling- more college, a workshop, a program so we can prove we know what we're talking about. We feel the need for certifications and degrees to be perceived as of value. I am not finding fault with that. However, I caution those of you who might have studied your subject for years out of the sheer joy of it- you already have plenty of knowledge to share.

Certification programs or degrees are such a part of our western world. But sometimes we are more focused on the piece of paper than the depth of the knowledge of the individual whose name is on the paper. Take this example of two different paths to study energy healing. In one school of energy healing, there are 3 levels of study. I took a level one, then practiced those skills on myself for 4 years to build my confidence that energy healing was real. Then I took a level 2 class and worked with clients for another 6 years before I felt ready to tackle level 3, which is the level where you become an instructor. So, I had 10 years of experience when I received a title of teacher/master. I see students take all 3 levels of classes in one weekend and then they too have a certificate as master/ teachers. I'm not saying they are not competent, but there is a wealth of experience that comes with time put into personal study.

When you go to art school, it is common to develop a style of art that is reminiscent of your teachers because your grades are based on pleasing them. When you study to become a teacher, your techniques to share knowledge are often similar to your professors, as they are your models. My point being, when you study with another, you can only learn what they have to share. They're showing you how to do what they did to achieve their goals and purpose.

When you study a subject out of passion or purpose, you often have a dedication to learning all you can. If I want to learn about gardening, am I interested that someone has completed a class and has a certificate of master gardener or do I want to spend some time with that soul who has been puttering in the dirt for decades out of love for the art of growing things?

My point here is if you are knowledgeable about your passion or purpose, don't resist sharing your knowledge because you don't have a degree or certificate. You are ready, and it is time. Even if you feel that your knowledge could be deeper, likely you know so much more than a beginner student. The knowledge you have, your desire to learn more, to seek answers to any question they have and your love of the subject will serve your students so beautifully- degree or no, certified or not. Of course, follow the rules of your career if licensing is required. I'm referring to non-licenses skills you may have.

The world is at a crucial time. It needs your help now. Yes, you can continue learning, but sharing knowledge is also a wonderful teacher. I learned a lot about what I didn't know when I began teaching. I learned that unless I have a deep understanding of a topic, I have trouble teaching it. I remember when I first studied religion. I was told that if I couldn't explain my beliefs to a 5-year-old, then I didn't really know and believe my subject. Repeating what our teachers told us to say isn't really enough. Take the knowledge from your mentors, but make it your own. A good way to do that is to teach, explain what you're passionate about to another person. That helps you make your unique knowledge your own.

So get to work in whatever way you can to share your passion, your purpose with the world. Share it with one person, someone you know, even family (although they can be the toughest audience.) If you are asked a question that you don't have an answer to, wonderful! Then you can say, "I don't know, but I'll look into that. What do you think the answer is?" Then the dialog continues with your inner wisdom communicating with the inner wisdom of another. Always remember the purpose is sharing. The purpose of connection is to exist with others in this world from a position of love and compassion. We're not in competition with other people. We are in community with them. Share your purpose, your love and compassion and the world can evolve beautifully.

"It is who we become that changes the world, not what we do. In other words, if we want peace in the world, we must have peace in our hearts."
-Sandra Ingerman, author of How to Thrive in Changing Times[34]

How does sharing from your inner wisdom help you?

I don't know about you, but I have an inner dialog in my head often. New ideas spin around in my mind. Concepts can get lost or unclear. To get some clarity, I write. This book is a clear example of me trying to make sense of a lifetime of busy thinking. Another crucial step for me is to try to explain my ideas/thoughts to another. Some times people don't "get" what I'm explaining and I might have to learn better ways to verbalize my thoughts. Most of the time, the other person says something that enhances or expands my idea. Oh!! That's fun. Share yourself with the world, not to be approved of… just because the sharing experience can often be so helpful.

How sharing from your inner wisdom helps the world?

Our world needs aspects of love and compassion to be empowered now. Share your wisdom in the spirit of uplifting, encouraging and supporting others. Combine your ideas with their ideas. Allow hope to grow. Light makes more light. Love makes more love. Share from your heart and others can connect better with their hearts.

this *journey*

23

Breathe- to listen and empower

What's the big deal with breathwork? I mean, we all know how to breathe? (smile) The big deal is that breathwork or conscious breathing is the most simple and effective method I know to shift your mood and your energy. No coffee or alcohol is required, just breathing. Before we get into the "hows" of breathwork, let's first talk about why breath is such a superpower.

A few chapters ago, in talking about energy, I mentioned that deeper breathing is one way to bring in energy. So breath can bring in life force energy when you need it. Nice!! So where does the mood alteration stuff happen? Let me tell you more.

It starts with our nervous system. We're looking at the aspect of your nervous system called the autonomic system. Your ANS (autonomic nervous system) manages processes, including heart rate, blood pressure, respiration, digestion, and sexual arousal. Our autonomic nervous system has two super powers or parts that we're concerned with-

- *Sympathetic nervous system- this system manages body processes that help in times of stress or danger. This system handles your body's fight-or-flight response.*

- *Parasympathetic nervous system- this system does the opposite of your sympathetic nervous system. It manages the rest-and-restore body processes.*

Fight-or-flight response kicks in when you feel threatened. For ancient humans, this is the power that helped them stay alive in a world where saber-tooth tigers wanted to eat them for lunch. Today, few wild beasts are going to munch on you on the way to work. However, fight-or-flight engages when you become angry or fearful. Now, instead of truly outrunning danger, we activate fight-or-flight when we fear job loss or some other failure. We become angry when someone pulls out in front of us because "they could have killed me or harmed my kids." For some of us, fight-or-flight can also include responses like freeze-or-please.

The body responds to your thoughts. It cannot differentiate what is really happening from what you are imagining might happen. In times of real or perceived danger, your body shuts down all systems that aren't essential to survival- digestion (including immune response), reproduction, excretion, growth hormone production, and tissue repair are all temporarily halted. Your visual acuity is up, breathing is fast and shallow to build oxygen in the bloodstream. Our thinking goes from seeing the big picture to a very narrow survival focus. Stress hormones are pumped out to help enable the body to respond to a threat. They increase blood pressure and heart rate, divert blood to the muscles, and speed your reaction time.

These changes are essential when you're physically running for your life, but when you're just angry (truthfully frightened) in traffic, you can't literally fight or flight, so all these changes in your body are not needed. In genuine life or death situations, when the stressor is resolved (the saber-tooth tiger wanders off after a more tasty prey), you collapse in the grass and breathe deeply. Your running burned off all the stress hormones and all body systems settle back into rest-and-restore mode.

That deep breath is a key here. Deep breathing signals your body's physiology that you are safe. The body then dials back all the fight-or-flight responses so digestion, immune response, healing and tissue repair come back online. Your creativity and ability to see wider perspectives return. One deep breath shifts your nervous system back to rest-and-restore.

In a healthy body, this shift from FF (fight-or-flight) to RR (rest-and-restore) happens often during the day, mostly unnoticed by you. However, if we landed in FF because of an imagined concern or even something as simple as an embarrassing event, when does the deep breath come to switch FF off? We can get in thinking loops of replaying "that dumb thing I did in front of everyone" or retelling the near miss car incident so our bodies can stay in FF for days, weeks. You get the picture. Our bodies must shift back to RR to function, heal, grow, and create.

This deep breath is an important habit for you to cultivate.

Conscious breathing is a powerful practice with many effective methods- some very restful, some very active which can help release stuck emotions. It is also important to understand that breath is a powerful tool to the spirit/energy aspect of you. Yes, breath connects your physical self to your spirit. My experience has shown me that breathwork affects the physical and it brings its energy into the mind and spirit. I found many, many references in sacred writings about the breath, but it really hit home to me in reading "The Miracle of the Breath," by Andy Caponigro[26] when I grasped that the breath IS spirit. There is a physical aspect of breathing, of course, that affects the body physiology and brings physical and emotional changes. But the energetic aspect of the breath is pure spirit. Caponigro shared these words from Kabir, a great 15th century poet and saint of India.

> "Are you looking for me? I am in the next seat.
> My shoulder is against yours.
> You will not find me in Indian shrine rooms,
> Not in synagogues, not cathedrals,
> Not in masses, nor sacred songs.
> Not in legs winding around your own neck,
> Nor in eating nothing but vegetables.
> When you really look for me, you will see me instantly.
> You will find me in the tiniest hour of time.
> Kabir says, "Student, tell me, what is God?
> He is the Breath inside the breath."
> -Kabir

I want to share the basic breathwork practice I teach. The beginning experience is incredibly helpful to many people and might be the only breathwork tool you need to stay calm, centered and balanced. This calming practice will signal your body to gently slide back into rest-and-restore mode.

this journey

It is easiest to practice breathwork lying down. I love to do it as part of my morning meditation. If lying down, you want your head to be on nearly the same level as your back. Propping the head up on too many pillows closes your airway down a bit.

Get comfortable. Have a blanket as you'll be still for some time. Lie on a padded or carpeted surface, or of course, the bed is comfy. You can begin this practice by just doing step one for 1-5 minutes or as long as you want. Get familiar with how that feels. You are going to practice watching the breath, noticing what distracts you and kindly calling the mind back to the breath. You will also be getting used to breathing consciously in through the nose and out through the nose.

Breathing through the nose is preferable if your nose works properly because it warms and filters the air coming in. If that doesn't work for you, then do what works.

Step one
Pay attention to your breathing- don't change it, just watch it. Allow yourself to become the observer of your thoughts while bringing awareness to your breathing. Notice how you feel as we begin the practice. Notice if your abdomen expands on the inhale. No need to change how you are breathing, just notice. Feel your chest expand as you breathe in and relax back down on the exhale.

You are receiving air and energy on the inhale. As you exhale, the waste gases leave, but the energy stays onboard. Just continue breathing, practicing being the observer of your mind. Watching where it wanders to, make a mental note of what your mind thought was important, then gently and kindly call it back. Remember that a wandering mind is perfectly normal. Sometimes my mind will stay pretty well focused on the breath and other days, it wanders continually. Don't let this frustrate you. You are training yourself to notice the mind and call it back, not training the mind to not wander.

Step two
Once you feel comfortable with conscious breathing, try to extend the exhale a bit, making your exhale slower or longer. Try counting slow and easy, counting the length of your inhale. Some of you can feel your pulse and that makes an excellent guide. We're not timing seconds here, we're timing relative length. So if your inhale lasts for 4 counts, then try slowing your exhale to 5 or 6 counts.

Slowing the exhale isn't easy at first. Initially, you're trying to limit the air flow by using your diaphragm. If slowing the exhale feels hard, try pursing your lips, like you're blowing through a straw. The restriction you make with the lips decreases the amount of air that can flow out, so your exhale takes longer. You are still inhaling through the nose but exhaling through the mouth. Or continue exhaling through the nose if you can manage the longer exhale that way.

This is the basic breathing practice in my breathwork workshop. The slower exhale is a great calmer for your body and mind. It stimulates the vagus nerve. The vagus is the longest nerve in the body and connects with most of your internal organs. It is the nerve that helps your body switch from fight-or-flight to rest-and-restore. A longer exhale extends the time of the calming exhale. The diaphragm, when fully contracted, also activates the vagus nerve. So if you practice a complete exhale, pushing all the air out on a few breaths, the movement of the diaphragm activates the vagus nerve. Even one deep breath signals it that you are safe and it passes the "chill out" message along to the rest of your body.

How can practicing breathwork help you?

For me, a slow calming breath is my number one tool to calm down, get grounded and centered. One deep breath can trigger your body to shift to rest-and-restore mode. In that place, even if your brain is still cranking like crazy, your body slows, your body chemistry shifts and those changes give you some space, some power to slow your thinking and redirect.

How can practicing breathwork help the world?

Well, honestly, some parts of the world have been using breathwork for centuries. However, you're learning and beginning to rely on this power to calm and settle yourself, and that helps everyone. If you're in a meeting and things get fiery, you can jump in with the others in fight-or-flight and add fuel to the problem or you can stay chill and be a force for cooling the situation. You don't need to say a word. Just breathe and the energy will radiate. You can help in a conference room, but you also are sending out calming energy to our world. Your bit of chill helps us all.

24

Your voice and its power

We all know the experience of someone expressing an opinion that hurts our feelings. There is at least some mild distraction and sometimes we feel real emotional pain. Some of us are more sensitive to this sort of energy. When we allow ourselves to be too strongly affected by what others say, it's a signal to strengthen our boundaries. In this chapter, however, I want to explore an area where boundaries can't protect us. Inside the boundaries is your safe space- your "you" zone. That is our nest, our comfort, and there is one person who is in charge of the energy flowing there, and that is you.

To keep your inner space safe, you must speak kindly to yourself. YOU MUST SPEAK KINDLY TO YOURSELF!! It really matters. When chatting with friends and clients about speaking kindly to ourselves, people will often say to me that they're just joking. They say that they don't really mean the unkind things or names they use for themselves. Well, let's talk about how seriously your body listens to you, especially when you're speaking about yourself.

Your voice, your vocal cords are tuned vibrationally to you. You can soothe, heal, and lull yourself to sleep with that special voice of yours. I understand that many of us don't like our voices. Perhaps you heard yourself on a recording or got pushed into singing something and weren't pleased with the result. If you're one who thinks your voice is awful, please pause for a moment and reconsider. We get into self-deprecating habits, saying we "hate" this or that about ourselves. The voice is a very common aspect of the self that people love to criticize and it comes from a fear of sharing ourselves audibly. In other words, it's a fear of singing.

On a side note, because it's a passion of mine, everyone can sing. Muscles control the vocal cords. Your ability to control the pitch or tone of your voice is a learned skill. Practice moving the muscles and you get better at managing them. Everyone's voice is beautiful, barring some damage that renders the vocal cords not functional. None of us is called to be an opera singer without training. Not all of us need to be a rockstar vocalist. I'm only asking you to embrace that sweet voice of yours and begin using it in your self-care. Singing is not some special skill reserved for a few select souls. All of us can make pleasing and healing sounds and words with our voices.

Your voice is tuned to your body, to your essence. What you say affects your body, mind and spirit differently than the callous words of others. Others say something unkind and we feel cut. But unkind comments from our own voice (audible or not) are perceived as truth beyond any doubt. We are wired to believe what our voice says.

Remember our exercise about the peach? We thought about the peach and our body had a real physical reaction. We're in that same realm here… what you say (aloud or to yourself), your body, mind and emotions will believe that it's true and respond accordingly. Please be kind to you. Many, many of us have fallen into the trap of making self-deprecating comments about ourselves. Whether we're criticizing the shape of our body, or our physical grace or the lack of it, too many of us are comfortable speaking unkindly to ourselves. Many feel that you should never speak well of yourself, as though it's bragging. Don't get caught in that trap and if you're there, let's start pulling you out of the quicksand.

Speaking kindly about ourselves, out loud and in our heads, is an act of self-compassion. Cheering yourself on has a powerful impact at an emotional level. "I can do that. I am capable. I will reach this goal!" These are all affirmations that can encourage you so much more than similar comments from others. Honestly, too often when someone offers us an affirming comment, we might smile and say "thanks" but on the inside we're saying, "Yeah, if you only knew me."

Take a deep breath. In this lovely life, you are the one cheerleader you can count on. You will always be with you. You even know exactly what you need. You can affirm, comfort, and support yourself more powerfully and perfectly than anyone else on the planet can. You might have grown up thinking your partner is supposed to be the one to support you, to know what you need. Surprise, they're humans and most can't read minds. Plus, your partner, best friends, co-workers are very busy with their own internal dialogue, hoping someone will come along and rescue them.

You are the one you can truly count on in life and that is not bad news!. You are the one to lift your spirits and inspire yourself to reach higher. Hooray!!! Because you know you can always be there for you. Sounds a bit sideways, I know, but in the dark of night, when you're feeling cold and lonely and the clock is showing single digits, it's you who is there. So wrap your arms around yourself right now and give yourself a hug and consider taking on the job of being your own cheerleader!

The voice is also audible sound, and sound is a healer as well. The simplest sound healing tool I know of is your voice. The easiest way to use it is to hum or sing. Some of us love to sing and others fear it, right up there with public speaking. Humming, however, isn't quite so terrifying. When you hum along with your favorite music, your specially tuned vocal cords caress you with their healing vibrations. Humming is self soothing, in other words, it's self-care. So is singing, if that's fun for you. So, explore adding a little vocalizing to your daily routine. Keep it in the car if you're feeling shy. Life is filled with positive vibes… hum along.

Beyond the self, your voice creates energy outside the body, too. We live in a world now, especially in the West, where it's rare to hear encouraging words. We love to complain. We're addicted to blaming. We criticize another for the smallest thing, throwing them under the bus because they haven't perfectly conformed to our expectations!

I remind you that the new world is here. It's time to let go of the negativity, the shaming, the blaming and the divisiveness in order to encourage the continued awakening of ourselves and others. I'm not saying the ever present "they" need to do this. We need to do it. I need to do it. If we talk negatively, we are radiating dense, tangled energy. We are giving our life force energy to exactly what we don't wish to have happen.

Whether speaking to yourself or anyone within earshot, first turn within. Pull your attention down from your busy, habit-ridden brain and look to the heart, your heart center. Breathe in to that central energy gate in the center of your chest, pause, and choose love and compassion. I'm asking you to find love and compassion within. Find it through thinking of someone or something you love. Think of it by picturing yourself in your favorite power or peace place. Embrace, surround, and completely swaddle yourself in that "happy place" energy. Only then, open your mouth and allow your love and compassion to flow out. Verbalize what you wish for, what you love, and stop spewing out your assessment of what's wrong or who's to blame.

Yes, this is a very tall order, I know. I fight it daily myself. Writing this book has been a stark realization for me of how my nature is not always to be encouraging to me. Writing a book is a new adventure for me. Almost every day when I sit down to write, my naysayer pipes up and says, "No one wants this. No one cares about this project. It's not good enough. It will never be good enough." Yep, there it is. That is what happens. Then I have to wrap my arms around myself, rock myself a bit and say, "You CAN do this. You ARE doing this. This book is part of your purpose. Even if it only helps one person, you are meant to do this. So GET ON WITH IT!"

When we allow ourselves to settle into old negative energy, we are seeking the old world. The 3D world, some call it, the lower vibration, dysfunctional world, which will not survive. It's that simple. If you want something better, then you must be something better. You want more love in the world, you must be more loving, more compassionate. The best person to practice with, because you're just so handy and in need of help, is yourself. The power you have to shift your life is tied intricately to how you speak to yourself, how you encourage yourself. So get to it. Listen when you're being critical. Listen to the words in your head and the words that come out when talking with another.

   "Talk to yourself like someone you love."–Brené Brown[27]

When you begin using your voice, your self-talk, to encourage, it might feel fake-ish. Try to find words you believe. "I did good!" works well for me. "I am the most amazing human ever" wouldn't fly for me. A sure solution to find my encouraging voice is to imagine a friend telling me they are feeling exactly how I am feeling right now. What would I say to them? Yes, then I say that to myself. Practicing these higher frequencies, expressing love and compassion regularly, makes it easier to opt for the light, to choose love. You are surrounding yourself with the higher energy of awakening, and that affects you and all who are near you. Again, we're not lecturing anyone about what they should do- we are doing it ourselves.

I wanted to close with the quote "be the change you wish to see in the world" often attributed to Gandhi. However, the truth is he never said that. Nice quote, but not his. However, what he did say, while longer and requiring focus, is even more beautiful.

> "We but mirror the world. All the tendencies present in the outer world are to be found in the world of our body. If we could change ourselves, the tendencies in the world would also change. As a man changes his own nature, so does the attitude of the world change towards him. This is the divine mystery supreme. A wonderful thing it is and the source of our happiness. We need not wait to see what others do."- Mahatma Gandhi[28]

How does using your voice in love and compassion help you?

Having an on-board cheerleader is so important in this changed world. Most people you encounter are filled with fear and trying to survive. Don't wait for them to lift you up. Do it yourself and do it often. Okay, do it all the time!

How does using your voice in love and compassion help the world?

When we choose a positive approach, it generates an elevating energy. That energy surrounds you and it floats to all those around you. Like dropping a warm stone in a bucket of cool water, your love and compassion warms the world, just a bit. Add your elevating bits to mine and those of millions of others in the world and together we all do make a difference.

this journey

25

True love is found through self-love

What the world needs now is love, sweet love. And, yes, loving each other, showing love, being love- all that is important. There is one love that gets overlooked. I'm seeing it as THE most important love. If you don't deeply love, accept, and honor ALL parts of you- if you're not willing to own and correct where needed, all your deep dark shit, then you can't really open your heart to love another. The love of self, accepting our perfectly imperfect selves, is a key to health and happiness.

> *"A lack of self-love is the root cause of our suffering, and most of our illnesses/diseases. But when we deeply nourish ourselves with our own love - the very energy and consciousness of our soul - we heal ourselves from whatever ails us, and receive a delicious life that feels like heaven on earth."* - Jerome Braggs, poet and medical intuitive[29]

In many of the chapters so far, there has been mention of self-love. But I want to dig deeper here, to truly get a point across. That point is- you are all you have.

Now, if that statement feels bleak to you, let me go further. You are the ultimate authority on you. You alone know what you need, want and dream of. You know those things if you learn to be still and listen to yourself or that small child who still dwells within you.

In an earlier chapter, I talked about labels from childhood and how they often still affect us as adults. We're also busy as adults getting new labels when we lose a job or a relationship. We might face financial or legal challenges. It feels easy to believe all those labels that point to our flaws, but don't. No one is perfect. Perfection is not part of the human condition.

this journey

I believe we come into this life to learn. The bumps in the road are part of those lessons. The times we fall short are just experiences, just lessons. They do not mean we are not worthy of love. Every being on earth, even those you don't like or might disagree with… all beings are worthy of love.

Our society has taught us through fairy tales, movies, romance novels and even commercials that each of us is looking for Mr. or Ms. "Right." When we find our "other half," then life will be complete. Every little princess thinks she'll find her prince (or princess) and live happily ever after. But when our partners leave or we never find "the one", then we can feel bereft, alone, and rejected. We feel not enough, not worthy of the love of another or at least that other person who ditched our relationship.

We are also taught that to love ourselves is conceited or wrong. This belief is ingrained in many of us. It's why we can't make time for self-care, because doing for others is noble and doing for self is "selfish." I looked up the definition of selfish and found that it is "an exclusive or exaggerated focus on one's own needs with no regard for another." The list of synonyms include: egocentric, egoistic, narcissistic, self-absorbed, self-centered, self-concerned, self-interested, self-involved, self-loving, self-oriented, self-seeking, self-serving. Can you see that many of these words are not at all negative? Of course, we don't always do for ourselves and never for community. But the general sense in our society is against caring for the self and therein lies the problem.

If we don't take the time to care for ourselves, to listen, and nurture ourselves, then who will? Who can? Who knows what we need or what will make our dreams come true but us? No one knows how we are feeling, how we sleep at night. No one knows what we see when we look in the mirror.

Our lives are so busy that it's hard to get everything done in a day. This bias against caring for the self leaves us always doing for others. Some would call this selfless. Selfless? Think about what that means. There is no self? This is not a compliment.

This new world is growing a structure that honors love and compassion. It's time for you to honor yourself as worthy of love, worthy of your love. Unless you begin to love and care compassionately for yourself, you will have nothing to give another. Wholeness comes when we feel complete within ourselves; when the love in your heart embraces all of you, "warts and all" as they say. Loving, caring, accepting yourself are the beginning. Then comes embracing your passions, and your purpose. Only then can you work towards building a life that honors all of you. When you find fulfillment and completeness as best you can, then you can stand with others and be an effective part of their world.

To truly love, you must first learn to love yourself deeply. Then the energy of real love fills you and surrounds you. Embrace that love and then you have something to share. That is the love that is lifting the world. Take a deep breath. Give yourself a hug. Go look in the mirror and say something to the effect of, "Baby, I do love you, you weird and wonderful human being. Let's go build a better world."

How does practicing self-love help you?

How can practicing self love not help you? Remember that it's your job to care for you so you can be your best you in this life of yours. Helping others is nice, but without self-care, you have little to give. It's like the oxygen mask warning you get on an airplane. Please complete your own self-care before attempting to assist others with theirs.

How does practicing self-love help the world?

Being an example of a happy, somewhat balanced human being can be a beacon to someone who is lost in self-sacrifice. When you are happy, healthy and filled with light, you shine, which elevates the energy of the world. The more light, the more this new world comes a bit more into view for others. Love yourself and help the new world achieve critical mass so it becomes clearly visible to everyone.

this journey

26

Your body is a natural healer

Hippocrates taught that healing is not the work of a physician but is caused by the *"vis medicatrix naturae"* (the natural healing power) within a human body.[30]

This chapter is often one people turn to first because they may have a physical or emotional challenge or they have a friend who needs healing. If that is the case, the information here can help you, your friend and all of us. You will find many alternative healing modalities that work with the body's innate ability to heal. I'm here to just share the one natural healing modality that I believe is the oldest.

You see, this chapter is more about your expectations and projections rather than a particular method of healing. Left alone, in many cases, our bodies can heal imbalances. This power to heal is assisted by getting appropriate exercise, eating healthy food, drinking clean water, getting deep sleep, soaking up sunshine, connecting to the earth, exploring and embracing emotional health.

The one most powerful way to help the body heal is to imagine, visualize, and believe that healing is possible. Why wait to be ill? Let's imagine wellness, wholeness, strength, and resilience every day. You're catching a common theme if you're reading through this book. I'm talking about our thoughts and projections again. Expecting to be well is a critical power in being well. And before we go too far, if you are ill, or have a loved one who is ill, I'm not saying they thought their way into their illness and can think their way out. Instead, I suggest that having faith in whatever healing modality they have embraced is very important. Combine that with good food, water, rest, movement (as permissible) and self-love. In these ways, you're doing all you can do to give the body what it needs to heal.

I have always believed that I can heal my body. Why would I believe that? I don't know. But that bit of wisdom is lodged deeply in my head, heart and gut and I'm glad for it. I have met others in this life who tell me similar stories. Many are people with no particular passion to make healing their career. But they know they can keep their body well. Most are aware of good practices in diet, exercise, hydration, sleep, and mental health. But the most important aspect that I have mentioned is that "they believe."

Modern western medicine operates on the premise that the body is like a machine in that if a part is malfunctioning, you fix or replace the part and all is well. Doctors prescribe remedies to relieve symptoms. When the symptoms resolve, then the patient is deemed well. Eastern medicine and many alternative therapies are more interested in how the malfunction occurred. Where is there an imbalance in the patient's life that might cause the problem? Is the patient emotionally healthy, socially connected, spiritually hopeful? Do they eat, move, drink, and sleep in ways that support a healthy, balanced body? Is the patient's social, spiritual, financial lives strong and balanced? Eastern and alternative healing seek causes or imbalances and work to resolve them, shifting the environment in and around the patient's body. The body, when relieved of the imbalance, has more power to move towards healing itself.

I recently read "Imagery Healing- Shamanism and Modern Medicine" by Jeanne Achterberg. Jean is a scientist. She and her scientist husband devoted their careers to studying the power of imagery, mental pictures, beliefs in the practice of healing. They focus on how imagery is used by shamans all over the world, and if you have a particular interest, the book is filled with so much powerful information that might help you build the power to believe in healing.

Shamans used sound, herbs, costume, movement, words and their important position in their society to help keep their communities healthy. A shaman will meet with a patient, then allow his/her spirit to journey into a higher plane seeking direction about how to help the sufferer. This journey is often completed as part of a ceremony, so the entire community is there to support the healing. Some traditions have the patient themselves journey into the spiritual realm, seeking information that will assist the shaman to learn the cause or the remedy to the patient's problems. Assisting the one in need to go find their own solutions seems especially powerful to me, as the patient is integral to this process. They personally gain the knowledge that will assist on their own healing path.

A critical element to healing the body is emotional health. Physical disease is often caused by imbalance in the emotions. A beautiful story of healing is Jerome Braggs, a medical intuitive, poet and more- who healed himself from anemia, pneumonia, pancreatitis, giardia, kidney failure, and AIDS after receiving a diagnosis of 7 days to live.[29] He writes that his inner concept of himself and his lack of self-love which grew from feeling unloved, contributed to his disease. When he received his diagnosis, he asked himself these questions, which I think are important for all of us to explore.

- *"Had I been happy with my life?"*
- *"Had I ever been my true self?"*
- *"Did I feel like I had lived my purpose for being here?"*
- *"Did I let the people in my life know how I truly felt about them?"*
- *"Did I feel good about who I was?"*

Braggs changed everything- how he cared for himself physically and particularly emotionally. It took time and was quite a learning curve, but he is happy and healthy today, 20 years later.

> *"When we truly love ourselves, all is well, all is coming, and all is delicious. But not a moment before."*- Jerome Braggs[29]

There are so many stories like Mr. Braggs'. I use him as a shining example because he has taken his experience as a calling and is sharing his healing experience, his skills as a medical intuitive to help others find healing.

We live in a world that doesn't encourage us to see our value- to accept, embrace and love ourselves. But if you've read this far through the book, you'll know how important I see self-love in every aspect of life. Sometimes we have things we'd like to change about ourselves, parts that should change for our health and well-being. It is important to remember; we don't wait to love ourselves. Instead, we love ourselves through the process of life and, in this case, through our healing process.

this *journey*

I have worked as a healer for many decades. I hesitated to use that title for a long time, as I can't heal anybody. What I do is create an environment of healing. I share knowledge with the client, ask questions, make suggestions if that feels welcome. The ultimate healing is really up to the client, not me. I offer healing energy and sound to a client. Most of my effort is spent helping them believe that healing is possible, informing them how they can assist their body in healing, how their efforts are truly working with those of their physician or other medical professionals. It's never an "us or them" thing. Healing comes when we create an environment, a community that helps us heal.

In healing work, it's most important to focus on the whole person/animal/plant. We're not trying to remove a problem. We wish to bring health, wholeness, meaning to the entire person, their spirit, and their environment. I imagine, visualize that they feel wholeness, peace, freedom. I remember that the challenges they are facing may serve a purpose well beyond our understanding.

Does healing work every time? No, my efforts and the efforts of individuals seeking healing do not always work the way we hope. Just as with modern medicine, not everyone recovers. That is not because they did anything wrong. It is because death is a part of life. Death comes sometimes early in life and sometimes much later, but it will come. Our society has created a sense that death should be fought or death is a failure. In my way of thinking, death is a graduation. You have fulfilled your life purpose, your lessons learned and taught. You are freed from the encumbrance of a physical self and fly free. I wonder if just accepting that reality might be healing in itself.

How does trusting your body's ability to heal help you?

I think embracing our body as a beautiful aspect of our wholeness is so important. Once you truly can love and inhabit this amazing flesh suit of yours, your awareness of it grows. You learn what feels right to you and when something feels off. Paying attention to imbalances and making adjustments are so important to our complete health. Consulting with others is often very helpful, too. But often we wait until some disease has set in, when perhaps the disease might have been avoided or mitigated by communicating with your body, mind, emotions and spirit every day.

How does trusting that your body can heal help the world?

The knowledge we gain about how to care for ourselves expands to how to care for our world. We all need healthy food and clean water. We need a safe, clean environment. We need love and compassion. We can help by applying these principles to others- humans, plants, animals, the air, the water... to our world.

this journey

27

Self-care is world care

Self-care is a term we hear often, but I want to talk with you about what it really means. When I say self-care, most people think about going to get a massage, a mani-pedi or getting in shape. Those things are lovely and they are caring. As I shared in the previous chapter, self-care is the care you give you, not just on the outside. You are a being that is physical and spiritual, visible and invisible, practical/logical and magical. Are you caring for the magical you? That is food for thought. Let's go deeper into self-care and the importance of extending that care to our world community.

Our medical system in the west is more sick care rather than self-care. We bop along through life doing whatever we wish, then a health crisis throws us into the medical system. It could be cardio-vascular, obesity, blood sugar issues, our mental health or so much more. We wait until there's a crash, then we go to the doctor and expect a pill to undo the damage so we can carry on. The COVID-19 pandemic taught us many things and one is that your local doctor or hospital can't put all things right with a pill or 20. We quickly learned that we play a powerful part in our own health and global health. Let's begin with actions we might take on our own.

Your body isn't a car. When a car wheel falls off, you can put it back on, maybe buy a new one and you're good as new. However, a human isn't a machine. You're an animal. You must be cared for in many ways to live a long, happy, comfortable, productive life.

There are seven aspects of self-care: physical, emotional, intellectual, social, spiritual, environmental and occupational. Each category is interdependent and influences the others. When one part of our well-being is out of balance, the other areas are affected as well. So, based on the seven aspects concept- your self-care involves diet and exercise, staying in touch with your feelings and your friends, considering your higher self and your body. You should have concern for how you interact with your environment, manage your finances responsibly so you can sleep at night and find work that isn't sucking the very life out of you.

Wow! It's a lot I know.

Self-care means that we can't choose to act like adolescents our whole life. At some point, we need to mature, step into our community and our purpose. One way to do that is to stay healthy. That's no fun… I hear you say. Yeah, well, being sick, broken and bored out of your mind at work isn't fun either. Welcome to engaging your higher self and serving our changed world.

The World Economic Forum discusses how current health challenges are affecting our world.

> "We need to move away from sick care and develop an integrated and universally accessible health model built on primary health care and public health support. The World Health Organization says primary health care is healthcare aimed at an individual's physical, mental and social well-being across their lifetime. It is people-centred rather than disease-centred. This includes empowering individuals, families and communities to take charge of their own health." [31]

There are more respiratory and allergy issues as global warming increases growing seasons. Food that is filled with processed ingredients and added chemicals abounds. The World Health Organization has formally stated that there is no safe amount of alcohol consumption.[32] Alcohol contributes directly to 5.3% of deaths and is a causative factor in some cancers, cardiovascular disease and Type 2 diabetes. These growing health challenges raise the cost of health care, lower productivity for the workforce and lower the quality of life for everyone globally. [32]

The adolescent mentality has us eating foods that are not good for our health. Many of us are not moving in ways that help body, mind, and spirit. It is common to gather with friends to ingest alcohol and sketchy foods when we could have all gotten together to go for a hike or enjoyed conversation and a healthy meal. We use products to clean our home and manage our yards that are toxic to us, to plants, insects and our water supply. When our relationships, sometimes our closest ones, aren't working well for either partner, we don't always seek help. Often, we ignore the problems until the partnership is gone. I know each of us has personal experience facing some of these situations and the ramifications.

Self-care is a big deal for each of us now. We all can choose to care for ourselves at least as well as we care for our pets. Take time for yourself. Move, breathe, hydrate, eat well. Assess your emotional state and if you need help with that, go get it. When you ignore your self-care until you face a medical crisis, there is so much damage done to your poor human animal. Love yourself enough to embrace taking healthier care of your body, mind, spirit, and this planet.

We must build the habit of checking in with ourselves frequently. Yes, it still takes some time and consistency, but self-care is do-able and should be manageable for all of us. If you're not sure where to begin, let me offer you a few of my favorites.

Morning wake up series

I start my morning with 12 deep breaths, with slow exhales. While still lying in bed, on my back with arms and legs relaxed. I think of this as time to oxygenate my system and also to keep mind calm, focusing on the breath or whatever interesting insights might float into my head. Any intrusive, unwelcome thoughts (worries) I just note and then call my mind back to the breath.

As you settle into conscious breathing, notice how your body feels. Bring hands up over the chest and rub palms together briskly, then place palms gently over your eyes, soaking up the heat and energy from your hands. Stroke your face gently from chin to the top of your head with open palms, using smooth sweeping movements.

Now place your hands over your ears. Again, just pause and soak up the energy. Then, using thumb and index finger or whatever feels right to you, massage your ears. Run your fingers over all the ridges and valleys on outside and underneath side of your ear, then use your fingers to massage the skin in front and behind, above and below your ears. Your ears contain acupressure points that connect with all organs of your body through your energy system. As you massage your ears, notice any tender spots. When you find one, just pause and gently massage that tender spot. Activating the point sends energy to an area of the body that needs it. There are maps of the ear's energy points which explain which organ is connected to which point, but honestly, I'm don't suggest we define specific problems. We're just using our body's built-in early warning system. Those tender places in the ear are just asking for attention and energy. I send that energy, attention and love to the tender points and often I'll find the tenderness diminishes. You can use the same method with your hands or feet. Explore reflexology if you'd like to learn more about this practice.

Pause after your ear massage and visualize a wonderful day ahead. This entire process will take only 5-10 minutes and can be done anytime of day.

I offer many self-care practices on my website. Explore if you wish. SuniMoon.net/readers/

How does self-care help you?

I think self-care helps me be a more mature human. My body, mind and spirit are at least as valuable to care for as are my pets. Take the time to figure out what you need. I need quiet time, movement times, nature times, rest times, healthy food and lots of pure water. I'm an adult responsible for the care and feeding of me. If I ignore my whole human animal- body, mind, emotions and energy- then there will be consequences. Be a big kid and take care of you.

How does self-care help the world?

In this new world, I anticipate living in a time when if I need safe shelter, good food and clean water, then I should be very clear on the fact that everyone else needs those same things. I can't pollute the oceans, pile garbage up without seeing responsibility for it. I can't allow the rainforests to be chopped down because of money because I know their survival is important to all of our existence. If I am part of a global community, then my care becomes world care.

28

Meditation your way

As we have wandered through this book together, meditation has come up several times. We explored watching our minds, redirecting our thoughts, and becoming the observer of that busy mind. I'm repeating myself, but it's important to me. Meditation is an integral part of life and it is within reach of everyone. So many people I meet think they can't meditate because they don't understand what the term really means.

The idea of seated meditation was brought to the west in the 1920s by Paramahansa Yogananda, an Indian-American Hindu monk, yogi and guru. But meditation isn't just from the east. Meditation is part of most spiritual traditions, in organized religion and well beyond. Shamans have used meditation since the earliest recorded history to connect with the spiritual realm. Given the wide use of meditation, there are many, many techniques and practices to explore. If the idea of connecting to a spiritual realm doesn't fit you, meditation is also a perfect way to calm yourself, to ground, to draw in energy or release energy, to shift your mood and connect to your best self.

Rather than go on and on about ways to meditate, I thought I'd keep this discussion very general. Meditation asks that we draw our attention to this moment. The mind can spend up to half its waking hours wandering around in time. We replay the past and predict the future with great regularity. If you are reviewing your past sweet, happy times, then that is wonderful. However, humans have a negative bias that wants to replay the not-so-nice times.

Negative bias means that humans remember and are affected more by events that impact them negatively than the ones that are positive for us. Facing two events of equal importance to us, we see the one with negative ramifications as being the more important, thus remembering or replaying it more often. This isn't because we're just "glass half full" people. In prehistoric time the world was filled with creatures. Some were large, with huge teeth, great strength and speed. Existing alongside all the creatures of the world were humans, not very large or strong, no protective fur, claws, or teeth. So, how might humans survive? Well, the negativity bias kept humans vigilant so they might not get eaten, and would survive to procreate so you and I can be here.

However, it's important for us to remember that there are no predators on earth now trying to eat us for lunch. At least they don't live in my neighborhood. We have turned our negative bias in a different direction in modern times and, at an emotional level, we are vigilant about so many things. Our fear-based society has raised us to fear homelessness, lack of food, lack of acceptance, poverty-maybe just lack in general. Meditation is one tool that helps us look at our negative bias, our non-stop vigilance, and helps shift our anxiety to peace. Meditation gives us space in our lives so we might focus our attention on how to love and express compassion.

Often when I talk about meditation with people, their eyes sort of glaze over. It's as if I'm suggesting they do "ONE MORE THING" in an already too busy day. The important message here is meditation is possible and different for every person. You don't have to sit on a cushion, cross-legged, and chant in Sanskrit. That's a beautiful groove for some, but not for all. There are many ways to put a calming, de-stressing practice, like meditation, into your life. Which of us doesn't need a simple, peaceful way to calm ourselves and reduce stress?

Mindfulness is a simple practice of setting your attention on this moment, assessing and accepting all that is right now. That might sound overwhelming, but I think of it this way.

- *Your life exists only in this moment.*

- *You can't relive that moment from yesterday.*

- *You can't live the event you're worrying about that may or may not be coming.*

- *You can only savor life in the now.*

- *You can only take action, live, learn, love, share, touch, laugh in this moment.*

If you aren't present and aware in this moment- it's gone. We miss too many of our precious life moments by rehashing old stuff or worrying about what's coming. While we're occupying our brain with the replaying and worrying, we totally miss out on the now.

Take a moment with me. Take a deep breath, pause, then let it go. Relax. At this moment, right now… you are fine. Likely you're clothed as you want to be, you have shelter, food- you are okay. You may have some challenges going on with your body or life but at this very moment, you're sitting here reading encouraging words and You Are Fine! Learn to enjoy your okay-ed-ness and don't waste this moment worrying about "what if I'm not okay" in the future. You are fine right now, relax. Breathe.

Mindfulness practices are tools that help us choose this moment. These practices offer ways to look at things we do every day n a different way. What follows is a part of my list of many ideas to bring mindfulness into your life. This is not your to-do list. It's just a list of ideas to try. One or more might appeal to you. If you adopt even one of them, you will begin creating a habit of experiencing mindfulness regularly. Remember, at this moment, you're fine. So get into this moment of your life as often as possible.

<u>Eating meditation</u>- Like many things in our day, eating is often a rushed event, shoveling nourishment in, while thinking about 50 things that need done after eating. In eating meditation, you've got several choices. You can try focusing on your meal with friends or family. Or you can make it a special solo time, perhaps with just a tiny special snack. Either way, the practice goes like this.

Look at your meal. Appreciate the colors, the textures, the variety of differences. Smell the scents coming from your plate. Even if you're snacking on a lowly raisin, pick that little gem up and have a whiff. Take a moment to imagine the journey your food has taken to reach you. Was it grown locally, or has it traveled from another part of the planet? Imagine how many people were involved in the growing, nurturing, picking the food and getting it to you. Take a few grateful moments, realizing that it's this food allows you to live, to keep your body strong and healthy. Then it's time to taste, but just a small bite at first. Allow just a tiny bit of food to roll around on your tongue, even noticing which part of your tongue picks up the flavor. Continue eating, noticing how a bite of vegetable might taste after a bit of bread. Thank whoever prepared this meal, as they have given you a lovely gift. Bon appétit!

this journey

Walking meditation- Take a walk. It's good for body and soul. Maybe take your doggie pal along with you. To work on mindfulness, set an intention for your walk. Think of things you're grateful for. Or notice how many shapes of leaves or colors of green you see. Listen to all the bird songs or other sounds that surround you. Notice people who walk past you and make kind eye contact with them and SMILE!!

Chanting meditation- Chanting is an ancient practice that can be performed just as the ancients did or with some updates. The practice gives you a phrase to repeat, often silently to yourself, but sometimes out loud. This is to keep the mind busy doing something in this moment. This simple repetition occupies only a small part of the brain. Your normally busy brain is chanting, but you can also find some stillness inside to explore. In time, you might realize you have forgotten to chant, but as you plumb the depths of your own mind and heart, you remain solidly in this moment. You can choose a phrase that comforts you to chant. Like, "Peace… peace… peace…" or "I'm okay… it's okay… we're okay…"

Journaling- I'm not sure everyone really understands how writing can put you so clearly in the moment. It works for me whether typing on a keyboard or writing something out by hand. You might choose to journal about the day's activities, accomplishments, or challenges. Some are drawn to write poetry. Consider writing a letter to someone far away or someone not even on this plane anymore. Before you write- pause, get comfortable and breathe. Consider your intention for writing. As you begin to write, stay mindful of the moment. Sometimes you will be surprised to see the words that appear on the page. These words often come from that wiser, higher part of you and can bring you truth, direction and encouragement that you need in the moment.

Ponder someone else's pain and think of one thing you can do to help. Our world can sometimes get very focused on me, me, me! "I'm so busy. I'm overwhelmed. I'm not appreciated," etc. It's often helpful to think of someone you know or someone in the news who is struggling. Imagine how they're feeling, how challenges affect their life. Then think of one thing you can do to help them. If it's someone you know, you might call or send a card. If the person is not someone you know, take a moment to imagine or visualize them rising above the challenge, or being freed from the problem. Spending moments bearing someone else's pain often makes our own familiar challenges seem much more manageable.

Breathing together- When leading meditation, I try to stay conscious of keeping the group comfortable. I don't ask them to match their pace of breathing with mine. People breathe at different rates, so I usually encourage them to breathe at their normal pace. But sometimes as we've been sitting together awhile and everyone is relaxed and nicely oxygenated, I encourage us to breathe together, breathing in the light or positive energy of the group, then breathing out our love to the world. This can be a powerful way to unite a group, calm, and bring attention into this moment.

Set an intention for the day- When you wake up, set an intention. Then recall your intention whenever you notice you're not living in the moment. Maybe write it on a note and tape somewhere you'll see it throughout the day. I've used the refrigerator, the car dashboard and my computer screen as handy locations for these reminders.

Create new patterns- You could try a series of "If this, then that" messages to create easy reminders to shift into higher thinking. For instance, you might come up with, "When I see the office door, then I take a deep breath," to shift into mindfulness as you are about to start your workday. Or, "If the phone rings, I take a breath before answering." Each intentional action to shift into mindfulness will strengthen neural pathways in your brain.

Driving yourself calm- Avoid road rage by focusing on mindfulness if you're stuck in heavy traffic. Deep breathe and relax. The situation is not in your control. Notice all the other drivers. You're all together in this. Likely it's no one's fault. Imagine that the tie up might be because of an accident. Visualize no one being hurt; send them light and love. Scan your body for tension and release as you can- rolling neck, lifting shoulders, shoulders forward, then shoulders back.

Mindfulness meditation can be practiced anytime, doing anything you wish. The point is to practice training your mind to live in the present moment AND when it wanders off, replaying uncomfortable experiences, choose to intervene and draw the mind back to this moment. There, you CAN meditate.

There is a much longer list of different approaches to meditation at SuniMoon.net/readers

How can practicing meditation help you?
For me, meditation shows me that I am separate from the continuous flow of babble that fills my mind. It also gives me the gift of knowing how to pull my attention into the now so I can really enjoy every precious moment of life.

How can practicing meditation help the world?
One more peaceful person, living in the moment, adds to our ability to see this new world. You are part of a community and your positive actions help all.

29

Going deeper

There are many times in writing this guidebook that I've felt like I'm being presumptuous. Like, in one chapter, I'm going to open a door to deeper meditation? As always, my goal here is to introduce a subject. If you like it, there are many other sources that can take you deeper. Let's see how this goes.

As we start in meditation, the focus is on watching your breath, directing your thoughts, and staying in the moment. Once I can manage some of those on a fairly regular basis, is there more? Yes. What more? Here's where I'm not sure how to describe this in a few words.

At our first level, we're trying to make space to listen. I want to hear my higher self. Until I can get beyond the incessant chatter of the busy mind, I can't find that higher direction. With practice, the chatter begins to die down for a few seconds and there is your opening. We can't expect when learning to meditate that we'll calm our brain down for long periods of time and float in bliss. Well, maybe sometimes we will. But mostly the breaks are short-lived and the chatter is back. It's most important that you understand that if this is your experience, this is normal! You're not a bad meditator, you're just retraining your brain. You're learning. Congratulations!

Now, as the chatter slows, start noticing small spaces that appear between your thoughts. There will be a bit of silence and once you notice it, it runs away and the busy brain is back. Don't give up. Watch for the next lull. When you see one, love it. Breathe deep and congratulate yourself on making progress. Wait for another and then try this line. "I wonder when my next thought will come?" I know this sounds counter-productive, like I'm inviting another thought. However, one struggle we have with going deeper in to meditation is seeing our mind as an enemy, as if it's an unruly child that needs to obey. When I learned this "next thought" idea, suddenly the pressure was off. A next thought is normal. I wonder when it will come.

Play with this concept and know that your tiny spaces of peace between thoughts can grow. Not rapid growth and not every time, but keep at it and keep your sense of humor. Maybe you can smile when that wily next thought arrives. Continue on. It's a sort of game you are playing with your thoughts. You are winning, but don't tell your brain.

These small gaps between your thoughts will grow. I imagine my thoughts as trees in the forest, all growing so close together. The gaps, the spaces between thoughts, become spaces between the trees. I watch those spaces get longer. They grow a bit wider until one day I can slide between the trees. I imagine that beyond the trees there is a silent pine forest. The needles are so deep on the earth that my footsteps don't make a sound. There is peace there… silent green lush peace. Then a thought comes and I'm back outside.

You might picture something different through your gaps. However it works for you, this is growth. The time I get to spend beyond the thoughts gets longer and longer. Sometimes I float away in there. Sometimes I can't get a break. Just depends on the day, and on how I'm feeling. Maybe it depends on how many cups of coffee I've had? Just know, there is another world between the thoughts. And once there, your job is just to listen- float and listen.

My goal in meditation is to calm and ground myself initially. I want my nervous system to find its way to rest-and-restore mode often. I want to navigate stressful times with some grace. But ultimately, I'm seeking my higher self. In the peace, I want to hear from the spiritual/energetic me. I have found that when I'm outdoors with my back nestled against the trunk of a lovely tree, that I can find the quiet space so much easier. I can take one deep breath, turn my gaze up into the leaves and blam, I'm there… lost in listening time.

What am I listening for? Depends on the day and the challenges. Often I just want peace and when I come back from my meditation time, I'll have a weird sense of knowing. There will be options and solutions available to me that I couldn't see before. Time in deeper meditation just clears the view for me. The "ah-ha" moment might come the next day or when I wake up in the morning. I believe I got the info during deeper meditation and it came clear in my conscious mind later on. The experience might work differently for you.

There are so many styles of meditation. Do look around at the options. What works for me may not fit you. Here are some basic styles.

1 Mindfulness practices. These are the experiences I've shared with you in this book. We keep our minds in this moment by trying to keep our thoughts on the breath. Some find watching the breath brings anxiety. If that happens for you, shift your attention to sensing the weight of your body on the seat, as it is your connection to grounding in the now. Mindfulness practices are a wonderful place to start, but also offer you the power of using meditation on the fly. One deep breath, checking in with how you're doing, offering yourself some comfort can happen in a meeting, while stuck in traffic or before you open your mouth to reply, not react, to something challenging.

2. Mantra practices. This style of meditation uses phrases to keep our mind occupied. You repeat a short sentence or even one word again and again. In time, you get "through the trees" and find some peace, and the mantra falls away. Traditionally, mantras were Sanskrit phrases. Maybe the most common would be "*Om Namah Shivaya*", translates as, "connection with our highest self requires prayer, love, grace, truth and blissfulness." For some, Sanskrit mantras are powerful but not so much for me. However, there are mantras that do work well for me. Try on "peace, peace" or "love love." Perhaps "receiving" on the inhale and "releasing" on the exhale. Repeat a phrase that means something to you in the moment, calling in some quality/energy you need or wish to shine out.

3. Guided meditations. Here someone is talking to you through the practice. It's a great way to begin, but for me, I can't get deeper unless the guide's voice eventually fades away and gives me some space to find my silence. Guides are effective in the beginning or when you are very stressed and need that gentle voice calling you in. Try different recorded meditation practices. When you find one that you love, work with it, but also allow yourself to practice on your own with mindfulness or a mantra.

4. Meditation retreats provide an opportunity to experience very long meditation sessions. Retreat centers are beautiful locations with peace, quiet and healthy food. You can get so deep in these beautiful protected spaces which remove you from your daily routine.

There are many more styles of meditation I have not mentioned. To me, most fall into one of the above categories but go look at them all. Or take what we've done here and build on it. You can find more meditation music and guided experiences on the website SuniMoon.net/readers

Channeling your highest self

As we work to bring a higher connection with body, mind, emotions and spirit, there are still times when the flow might feel more like chaos. Sometimes there are just too many thoughts in your head and it's hard to sort them out.

What to do? Automatic writing is a tool I use to connect directly with my higher self, or for some, with spirit guides or other energetic mentors. With pen and paper ready, the writer allows themself to relax into a calmer place, to slide attention from their busy brain down to the heart center and enter a meditative, channeling or journeying space. Each person is different and refers to this altered state of consciousness in their own way. The key is to not be thinking with your mind but to open to some other source of info, not the chatter box in your head. Automatic writing can be thought of as a form of channeling, but for me, I channel my higher self. We're stepping away from our busy brain and sliding down to the heart to listen for answers.

Automatic writing is a relatively young practice. Literacy and having pen and paper in the home wasn't so common until the late 19th century. The basic idea of contacting our higher selves or other spirits is age old. Automatic writing brought the idea of direct knowing to anyone who wished to explore. Direct knowing to me means a practice that anyone can connect to higher thought with no need for someone to "translate". These sorts of practices have always resonated with me as I get to have the experience myself as needed. I have a sense of knowing what information came in and I'm not relying on someone else's life experiences or preferences to translate a message for me.

Automatic writing came to us through the Spiritualist movement. You may know Spiritualists as Christian (or not) congregation who believe those who have passed on to the other side have messages for us. This practice was used and mis-used and became perceived by many as a stage illusion.

André Breton is considered by some as the "father of automatic writing," Breton was a medical doctor, working in a psychiatric hospital during World War I. Fascinated with his patients free and frenzied expression, Breton developed a way of using creative writing to channel the subconscious easily and directly. Breton later found fame as a poet, writer, and member of the Surrealist movement. Sir Arthur Conan Doyle, author of the Sherlock Holmes series, and his wife, used automatic writing to communicate with their son, who died in WWI. In the US, interest in automatic writing peaked in the 1920s. It faded away mostly during the depression but began seeing more popular resurgence in the mid 1970s when automatic writing and remote viewing were being researched by the US government.

While automatic writing still has skeptics, there are many who use it as a personal tool for getting in touch with their subconscious or higher selves. Its power to me is that it's simple to do, and it provides one more tool for anyone to connect with their spiritual aspect with no medium needed.

Today, we all have access to many "divination" tools. I have oracle cards which I use for personal readings sometimes, but I always have to look up the deck author's translation of what the cards mean. Of course, we also can just make a personal translation of oracle or tarot cards. Automatic writing to me just provides a clearer and easier message. The writings are not always deep or perfectly clear, but with a bit of practice, you might be surprised at the results. In my experience, I am seeking commentary from my higher self, but of course, you can seek insight from any spirit guide or ancestor if you wish. I will offer this one humorous caution that one of my teachers gave me many years ago. She said, "When you are seeking messages from those who have passed on, remember that dying doesn't necessarily make everyone wiser. Dear Aunt Tilly may still be a bit ditzy, even from another plane." When we access information from our higher selves, I feel like I can rely on it or often feel very comfortable with the information received.

Each automatic writing experience can be different. I generally pose a question to my higher self. Often the question is, "What do I need to know?" I write that question before sinking down into a more meditative place. Sometimes while writing the question, I'll get the answer and just keep writing. Other times, I go into a peaceful state and wait for an urge to pick up the pen. Sometimes automatic writing gives me an odd peaceful feeling of writing without thinking about what I'm writing. Or I feel like I'm almost watching someone else's hand write. For me, it's restful and fun.

The information received through automatic writing might make sense or not, especially when just beginning with the practice. I try to see the words as hints from my subconscious. Sometimes automatic writing brings me an idea that was just not on my radar at all. That fresh idea opens doors for me to look at things differently. Should I do exactly what automatic writing tells me? No, I think mature adults need to use all their faculties together to be the best they can be. So body, mind, emotions and spirit all together, like different voices on my board of directors. I do not think automatic writing is ever purposefully misleading, but be thoughtful when interpreting your writing.

It seems sensible to me to avoid automatic writing when you're tired, ill, or mentally or emotionally agitated. Don't approach automatic writing in a panic if you need decisive information immediately. Calm yourself, feed yourself, get hydrated, talk to a friend. Explore automatic writing when you're at peace. feeling balanced, and well.

I always reach out to my higher self. That contact is the most clear, safe and honestly so knowledgeable about my specific strengths, purpose and preferences. In all my experiences, I have always found that my best direction comes from within. Especially now, as our world has transformed to higher energies, we have more power, more intuition, psychic abilities, and connection to the wisdom of the universal or source consciousness. Your life experience or habits might direct you to guides or angels. If that is your most trustworthy path, then do you. I can't make specific recommendations on those choices, but I imagine you can. Reach out to whoever you might normally call for guidance. But I also want you to consider finding your truth within. There is something so powerful to me of knowing that the connection to all wisdom is right within me. I don't need to call out for some faraway entity to help. This is also the easiest connection to make. Just try it, then do what is best for you.

How to prepare for your automatic writing session

Automatic writing is a form of meditation and preparation is similar. Breathe- a nice long full breath in through the nose and out through nose or mouth is a great warm up. Get comfortable where you intend to write. I suppose a desk is most common however, 90% of the time, I do it in bed before going to sleep. Yes, sometimes this means I miss my automatic writing session by falling asleep, but sleep is pleasant too? (smile)

Get comfortable. Have your pen and journal handy. I write my question down in the journal. Again, I often use "What should I know?" Then I take some nice full breaths. It's the same practice we've used to slide into meditation. Take a few breaths, then ask your question in your mind.

Allow your attention to float down from your head (busy brain) into your heart center area. Notice how it might feel different focusing here. Often people notice they feel calmer and things just slow down a bit when we breathe into that heart center. Then, settle into natural breathing and watch your thoughts. You are waiting for some direction to come. This is a practice that gets easier when we continue to develop our skills, so don't push things.

Write whatever pops into your head without criticism. We will commonly think, "This isn't working" or "I'm doing this wrong." It IS working and you are doing it right. It's just a practice that sometimes takes time. We are again working in the spiritual, invisible, magical realm.

Write what comes to you. Messages don't come in full, complete sentences with proper spelling and punctuation. Just write. Sometimes I get one word- like "GREEN!" I try not to think, "Green what?" I just write green, then close my eyes and keep listening. Your writing might be messier than you're used to. You might not be writing on the lines. Just write. Keep breathing and write as long as there is info to write or until you wish to stop.

The first time you try this practice, choose a place where you might not be disturbed for 30 minutes or so. In time, it's easier to learn to filter out outside noises, or the sounds of others in the house. I can do this on the train easily, because I've practiced a lot. Don't make this too hard. Everything doesn't need to be perfect. If 5 minutes feels like enough, start there. This is your practice.

Some people write digitally. I like handwriting and I think it's easier to learn the practice that way but as always, do you.

Practice

1. Gather your equipment. I have a favorite journal and a favorite pen. Get two pens, just in case. You can write on anything with whatever utensil feels good to you. Crayons might bring out your inner child. I find a nice gel pen is smooth and silent. Use what appeals best to you. I keep water handy. You might want a favorite crystal or six nearby. Set up your desk a bit like you might set up an altar. Stones, light, aromatherapy… whatever feels nice to you.
2. Clear your writing space.
3. Check that your chair is comfy and that you are warm enough, as you'll be still for a while.
4. Sit down, stretch a bit, roll your neck, have a drink of water.
5. If you have any worry about contacting something negative or feeling unsafe, say a little prayer- holding safe space for yourself, shining your light, asking for connection with only kind, wise sources if you're not working with your higher self. Visualize a fun, informative experience.
6. Think for a few minutes about what to ask. Write your question down in the journal.
7. Start your breathing- calming, grounding and filling yourself with energy.
8. Switch to natural breathing and listen. When you get something, write it down. You might get one word, or three words, or a sentence. Then listen some more. You might get page after page. Keep writing as long as you are enjoying the experience.
9. Thank your higher self or thank whatever spirit you connected with. Be grateful for a fun experience. Breathe a few more deep breaths. Ground yourself to the earth and feel into your body. You're back!
10. Read what you wrote. Or in my case, I go to sleep and read it in the morning.

this *journey*

If you don't succeed on your first try, don't worry. Try again another time. Sometimes I get something. Sometimes, I take a nap. This is a fun, relaxing practice. Practice, get it?

Sometimes you might get pictures or sounds. You might see a scene acted out. Draw or describe what you're seeing. If you're hearing a sound or a tune, describe that. I get melodies often and just hum them into my phone. Often you might find that your written message makes little sense. This is more common that you might think. I keep all my automatic writings in one journal so I can go back to previous writings. Sometimes a message comes in parts- some today, some tomorrow.

A very common reaction is, "Am I just making this all up?" The answer is no and yes. No, you're not just making it up, it's coming to you for a reason. And yes, it's a sort of magic, wonderful, playful process and there can be a certain about of creativity involved. Some people might say we are making all of life up. So don't worry. As you practice, you might find a little feeling of urgency or anticipation when you see your journal on the desk. That feeling tells me there might be something waiting to come through. Have fun with it.

31

The power of nature and forest bathing

In my lifelong study of spiritual practices, there is one aspect that shines brighter than most anything else for me. That is the power of our natural world. Since I was a child, nature has been my playmate, my shelter, my sedative, my teacher.

I moved back to Ohio in the early 2000s to be near family. My dad was older, my sister missed me, and the cost of living there was considerably easier to keep up with than in Denver, Colorado. I bought a house, moved home and tried to begin the next phase of my life. But it wasn't a peaceful transition. Small town Ohio didn't welcome my work as an energy and sound healer, meditation and breathwork instructor. My hometown was vastly less open and progressive than Colorado. My dad died seven months after I moved. I felt stuck, lonely and sad often. I shared my home with a dog and a cat. That dog, my Buddy, took me for a walk every day. There was a small park with a pond full of geese and huge old sycamore trees near my house. Every day, we'd go wander that park and I got in the habit of leaning on this one particular sycamore. Somehow, I found a spot where I could lean and that tree fit every contour of my back, like two puzzle pieces clicking together.

I leaned on that tree daily and began talking to it, mostly in my mind... mostly. I talked out all my frustrations. I cried so many tears into that tree's beautiful bark. For 7-8 years, I visited my sycamore therapist. I would talk when I arrived, but once I had said enough, I just leaned in and listened. Answers somehow came to me. Comfort flowed from that tree. I remember thinking, "I wonder if trees have chakras because I think ours are in direct alignment."

As a child, I spent a lot of time in nature, but until I moved to Colorado and began studies of healing practices, I neglected my love of nature. As all people, I've been through tough times in my life, but I chalk it all up to lessons. Once in Colorado, I felt the mountains calling to me and reconnected with nature. But the move back home to Ohio took me from those wild, beautiful mountains and I found myself standing in a dinky park with sidewalks covered with goose poop. However, my one tree was so much more than enough to sustain me, support me, and guide me.

In 1982, a term "forest bathing" was first used in Japan. The practices are much older than that. But this term brought fresh interest and research in the age-old wisdom. Soon media was telling us to spend time in nature for our physical and mental health. Richard Louv published a book, "Last Child in the Woods" in 2005. Many people credit Louv, a journalist in San Diego, with starting this movement and he coined the term Nature Deficit Disorder. He said,

> *"This subject was virtually ignored by the academic world. I could find 60 studies that were good studies. Now it's approaching and about to pass 1,000 studies, and they point in one direction: Nature is not only nice to have, but it's a have-to-have for physical health and cognitive functioning." - Richard Louv*[33]

In 2010, Clinton Ober wrote "Earthing: The Most Important Health Discovery Ever?" Ober shared that direct contact with the earth, with soil on our bare feet, made significant improvements to our health. I had read Warren Grossman's book "To Be Healed by the Earth" when it came out in 2007, so I was already napping in the grass with the ants and the worms. Since then, there has been extensive research in to all modalities of connecting to Mother Nature. These studies have shown that time in nature can reduce stress, anxiety, depression and anger. Your experiences in the woods can lower blood pressure and stress hormone levels, calm the nervous system, improve immune system function, lower inflammation, increase self-esteem, and improve your mood.

Beyond the science, time in nature is a way for us to connect to our spiritual side. Wandering through tall trees, waving grasses, colorful flowers and buzzing bees… we can't help but notice that there is so much life in our world. Nature is resilient despite our lack of care and consideration for her. Our tree friends stand tall in one place, overseeing the world around them. They brace for the winds and soak up the sun and rain, producing a green canopy in summer and gracefully releasing it in fall.

A most astonishing thing about trees is how social they are. The trees in a forest care for each other, sometimes even going so far as to nourish the stump of a felled tree. Perhaps these stumps are the parents of the trees that make up the forest of today. A tree stays connected to other trees through an underground network of roots and fungi that allows sharing of information and material. Scientific research aimed at understanding the astonishing abilities of this partnership between fungi and plants is growing. Trees share food and communicate to create a microclimate that allows them to thrive. Isolated trees have far shorter lives than those living connected in forests.

While you may not consider yourself outdoorsy, making time to breathe fresh air, feeling the sun on your back and digging your naked toes into the soil is a sweet, sweet way to meditate, to calm and to connect to a greater world than you'll see on the news.

Many cultures see our planet as a mother, a provider, a nurturer. She is filled with energy and is as much alive as any human being ever can be. She has a spirit, just as you do, as the trees, and the grass and the bees do. You might visit your natural relatives more often. Stop and commune with the beauty all around you, whether in a city park, in your backyard or visiting wider open spaces. My meditations outdoors are so efficient, healing, and filled with energy. I always come back from a hike more hopeful, energized and clear. Seeking your higher self? Go ask a tree. You'll be surprised at how much you can learn by placing your back against bark and hanging out for a bit.

Suggestions for nature bathing/ meditation/ communing

<u>Take a walk-</u> breathe naturally, but observe your breath as you set out. Try counting the length of your inhale and exhale. Check it again when you're nearly done with your walk to notice change not only in breathing but also in how you are feeling.

<u>Engage all your senses-</u> How many shades of green do you see on your walk? How many birds or insects are singing to you? Notice the smells of earth, air, and flowers. Engage with the different textures of bark on the trees .

Walk the dog- Take your pet friend with you for a walk and observe what your dog notices. What draws its attention? What excites your fur friend and what seems to calm it? Can those things have the same effect on you?

Lie in the grass- Look at the sky and if you're really lucky, there might be clouds floating by. Some might form recognizable shapes. Try taking intrusive thoughts out of your head, hold them on the palm of your hand and blow them up to the clouds to carry them away.

Walk with a friend in silence, at least for a few stretches of your walk. Then pause and share your favorite sights, sounds or smells.

How can bonding with nature help you?

The real world isn't on the computer or cell phone screen. The real world isn't in a book. My favorite "real world" is taking a walk in nature. I breathe cleaner air, hear vibrations and songs created in the moment. I am one creature in a landscape of millions of creatures- in the air and below the earth's surface. Many of these creatures have been around years before I was born and will be alive and well when my existence has faded into memory. Find your place in the community of nature. Be a mature adult and serve that community.

How can bonding with nature help the world?

Nature isn't part of me. I am part of nature. I am a component, a being among millions. I must serve nature and help her along if I expect her to continue to help and support me. Nature isn't here to serve me. I am a tiny servant of hers.

32

Creating ritual and ceremony

When I studied with the Lakota tribe on their reservation, their powerful sense of community was something I had not experienced before. The people ate together, shared ceremonies, cared for their community. They really knew each other. In my life, we wave across the fence at our neighbors. Our family gathered together to celebrate holidays- it's Christmas, it's Easter, it's Thanksgiving. We met to eat and catch up, but mostly we shoveled in the food and talked about things that didn't interest me. "How about those Browns?" Yeah, no.

Ceremony on the reservation was so different. People had to be clear and ready for the event. They abstained from alcohol for days before. Some didn't eat the day of the ceremony. Your body had to be clean. Your mind should be clear. There were special clothes to wear. You prepared yourself inside and out for the ceremony.

When we gathered, it was a time of awe. I knew something special would happen, and I was so grateful to be included in the event. It was a time when I was acutely aware of my physical self- the darkness, the heat, the waves of scents from the herbs being burned on hot stones, the small bit of cool air I found as my face laid on the earth at the edge of the lodge. While our bodies might suffer, our spirits were the stars. As we sat in a darkened space- faces, genders, roles faded into the shadows. We were energy connecting across that pit of hot coals- reaching to each other, reaching up to the above and down into the earth. We connected in love and in awe. These times of ceremony showed me how to be wholly me- body, mind and spirit.

Sound good to you? Maybe seeking a cool breath under the edge of the lodge sounds rough, but many of us seek what ceremony and ritual offer. We want a special moment to float, to seek, or to wonder/wander. We want to feel and experience more than the mundane routine our lives can provide.

Ceremony and ritual are such lovely, even mysterious terms. Allow me to help define them. Truth is, definitions are not so important. Spirit will not step back and say, "Oh, I'm not helping here because your terminology doesn't suit me." Ritual and ceremony are creative processes. Just as there's no one right way to create a beautiful piece of art, nor is art's beauty agreed upon by all, your ceremony or ritual is yours to birth. Have fun with it.

In the book "Awakening to the Spirit World", Sandra Ingerman[34] opens the chapter on ceremony and ritual this way.

> *"Ceremonies and rituals are performed to honor the spirits, to celebrate life and changes in Nature, to acknowledge rites of pause, to give thanks and to create change. Performing a ritual or ceremony creates transformation." -Sandra Ingerman*

Transformation is such a powerful word whose meaning can include: healing, growing up, growing old, changing circumstances, supply, or weather. Transformation involves the physical but also the emotional, mental, or spiritual. Ceremony affirms our connection, our very essence, as empowered beings. You don't have to hope you're doing a ritual right. Your intuition of how to celebrate an occasion is always right if it's based in love and compassion. Your essence is part of spirit/energy so is always connected to a greater source. Ceremony and ritual are conscious efforts in the physical/visible world to connect to our magic. Sit back to relax and have fun with it. I never thought twice when I was five and making smoke signal ceremonies to the clouds if I was doing anything wrong or right. It just was me and that was/is inherently good.

In my understanding, a ceremony has a predetermined structure and goal, which you create. You set an intention and want to include certain things to reach a specific goal. A ritual, on the other hand, is more free form. We still set an intention, but the result is not under our control. Ritual is more an idea of handing the situation off to the spiritual, invisible, magical aspects of life and they get to surprise us. In ceremony, you direct what you wish to happen- "we'll sing, then we'll arrange some stones, we'll write our wishes, then dance and close by reading this poem." In ritual, we ask spirit to drive, then sit back and watch what happens.

Ceremonies are often arranged so a group can take part, creating a path so community can achieve a purpose together. Ceremonies can include group meditation and prayer, group dancing, sharing a feast or joining in a pep rally. Weddings are a ceremony. All gather to listen to the prayer, the sharing of vows, exchanging rings, a blessing, a kiss. We've all attended enough weddings to understand that there are many ways to accomplish that goal. All are valid and good when based in love and compassion.

In ritual, we set an intention. We call on our spiritual selves, our higher wisdom, our ancestors to help us with what we need. Then magic takes over and we don't really know what the outcome will be, but we're hoping for something wonderful. Asking for healing is a ritual practice. We know we can't direct exactly what will happen, but we trust it will be beneficial to all. Some healers make the error of focusing on what is wrong with their client. We should not focus on what is broken. Healing works towards bringing energy to the whole person- body and spirit. We work for their wholeness, peace, freedom. We know that the challenges they face may serve a purpose beyond our understanding.

Rituals might be habitual tasks we do regularly, alone. We may visualize health and happiness in our home. We honor spiritual aspects that support us. I burn a sage leaf before I tackle a task just to clear myself and the space. My dog has to spin around 3 times before she'll come in the door. I don't understand her ritual, but I choose to honor it. Why not?

There are no clear rules with ceremony and ritual, just some general understandings. Don't get slowed down trying to do the right thing. Allow yourself to be excited by the possibilities. We don't hesitate to dream. Many of us pray with great freedom. Look at ceremony and ritual as ways you might help connect your physical world with your spiritual world, allowing the visible and the invisible to dance.

> "That, I think, is the power of ceremony. It marries the mundane to the sacred. The water turns to wine; the coffee to a prayer." - Robin Wall Kimmerer, "Braiding Sweetgrass"[35]

You can easily create ceremonies and rituals. You don't need an officiant. You are the minister of your own needs and perhaps the needs of others. We all can be part of ceremonies to give and receive, to connect and learn. So, where to begin? There's no rule book for having a ceremony. Here are some elements of ceremony that help me.

1. Set a strong, clear intention you wish to accomplish.

2. Have a plan of what to include in this experience- this music, this crystal, this material to smudge, these instruments. This becomes a to-do list to prepare so you don't have to go running in the middle of your practice to find a lighter or whatever.

2. Stay focused through the practice. Don't allow yourself to become distracted as that disconnects you from your energy, your spirit. I try staying more in my heart center focus than in my head. The head wants to do everything perfectly. The heart will help you do things truly and with love.

3. Create a state of harmony in this work. Harmony and peace in the place, in the altar if there is one, in the group, in the timing. Be open and things will work out just like they are supposed to.

4. Consider simplicity, especially as you begin this work. Some ceremonies can be more involved. However, some shamans are known for rituals that are short and sweet, getting to the point- open the door, connect to spirit, state the intention, honor those helping and give thanks.

Intention

Just a few words about intention. Sandra Ingerman, in her book "Medicine for the Earth,"[34] shares a story of a woman who set the intention of finding a rich husband. The woman laughingly shared this story with Ingerman as she introduced her husband, Rich. They were poor, but happy.

Be clear about what you want to accomplish. Use words that explain exactly what you need. Saying you want your heart center to open can mean you want to be more loving or you're inviting heart surgery. That's a sort of joke, but many have shared that they got what exactly they asked for. I don't. wish to make you fearful, but to encourage you to really dig into what you need. If I'm seeking companionship, should I ask for a life partner, a pet or community? Look into your own hopes and dreams. You might insist that your daughter and her husband quit fighting, when if they continue to fight and part ways, then they both might find true happiness.

This train of thought carries over into healing. Initially, you might think that you should ask for a disease or malady to be removed. Obstacles fall into our paths, so we learn, grow, and evolve into higher, wiser beings. I've worked with many people who tell me that their experiences with cancer saved their lives by forcing them to change. So when doing healing work or setting our intentions, try allowing your attention to slide down from your head to your heart and make simple requests.

- *May we find healing on our path (without defining healing of what.)*

- *May there be peace in the world (rather than wishing ill for one side in a war.)*

- *May they embrace the power of spirit in their life.*

- *May I connect with my own higher wisdom and purpose.*

Aspects that can be included in ceremonies

- In some traditions, it is common for everyone to bring something to include on the altar or center space in the ceremony. This isn't necessary, but you can ask folks to bring a favorite crystal or photo or special something to put on the altar during the ceremony. They then retrieve their item to take home with them when the ceremony is complete.

- A song or statement can open the ceremony to greet the participants and make the purpose clear

- Offer gratitude for those attending in physical and spiritual forms

- Calling to aspects that you feel might contribute to the event. In some traditions, they call in spirits from 4, or 6, or 7 directions. Some traditions look to the elements- earth, air, fire, water, spirit (with

this journey

many derivatives to this list.) I feel I bring the all-that-is with me. I simply call our attention to the physical and spiritual, the visible and invisible, the practical/ logical and magical.

- Allow a time of blessing and connection. Some use a method of purifying, like sage or other smudging. I don't like to think we walk around "dirty" but I love the scents of sage, cedar, sweetgrass and others. I do this part to honor traditions I learned from. I often use sound here too, using bowls, or bells or playing music so that all in attendance (and sometimes that's just me) get ready or be open to walk thru a "doorway" into the practice. This is a time to accept the blessings of being together, of the smells and sounds, to connect and ground to the earth below and the sky above. The burning and sounds, the grounding and connecting, remind us that the energy created will be shared with the world.

-The body of the ceremony/ritual might include: allowing all to speak in turn, dancing together, sharing a reading or a song. You might share a meal here or lie on the ground in silence. One tradition I trained with would pass a pipe around, others pass a talking stick. You may all go on a journey or sit in meditation. Consider how you might best accomplish the intended purpose of this ceremony.

- Closing the ceremony brings everyone's attention back to purpose, calling them back to the now. Express gratitude to all. Some release the spirits or powers they may have called in. Take some time and allow everyone to reconnect with the now and the "normal."

I want to include a list of ideas- purposes for your ceremony or ritual and different aspects or activities you could do. I am laughing because I could probably write this chapter for the rest of forever and not get done. I will include some suggestions here. More suggestions at SuniMoon.net/readers

Reasons for ceremonies and rituals: holidays, seasons, phases of the moon, phases of life, for couples, a community or family, for goals, a job, a blessing for a new home. Reasons can be as simple as a pause during your morning coffee, or a deep breath to calm yourself as needed.

Just do you. Sit quietly, play your favorite music, sip your tea, hum a tune, say a prayer, talk to yourself or a departed dear one, repeat mantras or affirmations or savor the sweet silence. Your ceremony or ritual is yours. It can change every time, it can remain the same for a lifetime.

You are carving out space for the sacred in your life, strengthening the connection in you of physical and spiritual, visible and invisible, practical/logical and the magical. Enjoy.

How can creating rituals and ceremonies help you?

This is just one more way to remind yourself that there need be no barrier between what is sacred or "higher" and your physical self. You need no officiant or priest to conduct your ceremonies and rituals. You are connecting with your higher you and whatever else you intend.

How can creating rituals and ceremonies help the world?

I find experiencing or learning about rituals and ceremonies of others to be fascinating. People are often happy to share their ceremonies with you if you ask in a loving way. We have so much to learn from one another. Experience the ways of the other with your focus on the experience, not with an urgency to tell them how you'd have done things differently.

this journey

33

Sound - a healing energy

Sound is a lovely universal language, a current that flows to lift and shift. We think of music as coming to us through our ears, but the vibration of music and all sounds flows to every cell in our body. Sound changes everything. Vibration is a characteristic of being alive. We all vibrate- humans, animals, plants, stones, water, air, the earth, the cosmos. Beautiful vibrations all around.

We resonate down to the cellular level with many frequencies and harmonics in our body. I read that each of our cells is singing its sweet song to all the cells nearby. Our personal vibration is affected by many things- emotions, temperature, how hydrated we are, how much rest we've had, barometric pressure, quality of our food... who knows all the ways we can shift our vibe.

Sound is a very scientific aspect of life. Some of our body's vibrations/ frequencies can be felt and measured as part of a health assessment. Doctors measure electrical activity of the heart and mind. We can feel our own pulse, creaking of our joints, rumblings in our gut. There is a pulse to our cerebral spinal fluid, and electrical impulses power our nervous system. All these are vibration, some audible as sound to our ears and some more subtle.

Your vibration shifts with your energy levels, so it's easy to imagine that if you're feeling depleted, your vibration will differ from it might be when you're feeling 100%. I'm not suggesting there is one optimum vibe to aspire to, just that your vibe shifts and you feel differently when the vibration changes.

Using sound as a healing or calming modality comes from ancient times, but it has a modern scientific basis. In physics, we can study the practical applications of resonance and entrainment. Resonant sounds or vibrations are those that appeal to us, that we are drawn to. Entrainment is the phenomenon that occurs when one vibrating entity affects the vibration of those nearby. If I strike a tuning fork near another fork with the same tuning, the un-struck fork will begin vibrating, entraining to the one that has been sounded.

If you've ever visited a cuckoo clock store while traveling in Germany, you can't help but notice that every clock in the store is ticking in unison. Every pendulum is swinging in alignment. You might imagine that the store owner must time the clocks as he hangs them, but no. Cuckoo clocks entrain to each other and tick together. This same marvel comes when women live together in the same home- their menstrual cycles will often synchronize.

Sounds vary by frequency, often measured in hertz (symbol: Hz). Sounds have a waveform. The frequency or hertz is the number of wave peaks per second. This is a measurement of highness or lowness of sound, not loudness. An average human voice measures 1000 Hz. The purr of a domestic cat averages 25-150Hz. Humans can hear 20 Hz to 20,000 Hz (20 kHz or kilohertz)

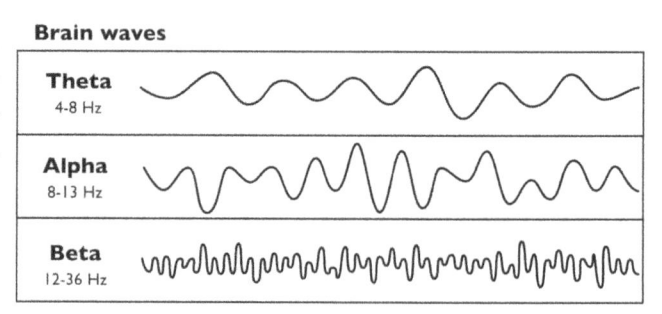

Brain waves

| **Theta** 4-8 Hz |
| **Alpha** 8-13 Hz |
| **Beta** 12-36 Hz |

Without going too science geek on you, let's talk a bit about harmonics of sound. I play crystal bowls which produce a very simple, one note tone- steady and clear. If I play two bowls, you hear two notes steady and clear, but you'll also begin noticing waves of sound, louder and softer sounds, pulses and beats.. The vibrations of the two bowls merge and create new sounds or harmonics of their own. So imagine your vibrating body lying peacefully while I play the bowls near you. The vibration of the bowls and the vibration of your body together create fresh sounds and new vibrations for your body and spirit.

To me, sound healing has to do with the fact that your body is always innately seeking to find its optimum vibration because your body is a natural healer. So when I offer sounds, harmonics to the body, your body has the know-how to combine with those sounds in ways that will assist it in returning to optimum vibration. This isn't a conscious thing. It is a skill of the higher self, the spirit, and the autonomic nervous system. Sound can assist your body in finding its optimum vibration and health. You resonate with those tones and frequencies that your unique body needs.

Some teach that there is a certain frequency intended to fix or heal a particular imbalance. For example, a 512 Hz tuning fork is used in modern medicine to check for conductive or sensorineural hearing loss. In the alternative healing community, that 512 Hz tuning for is advertised as resonating with the heart chakra. 528 Hz is promoted as the "love frequency." Google just told me that 639 Hz is good for sleep, to heal your heart and to create better relationships. I'm not saying these statements are untrue. They could be good places to start with sound for a beginner. Sound will affect us all differently, in different ways, on different days. It's my intention to help a client that leads me to choose a particular sound or most often, I just play a wide range of frequencies so my client's body, mind and spirit can soak up what is needed.

I create sound experiences to help people rest in a range of vibrations- to feel more calm or energized, to meditate, to drift off on a shaman's journey, to connect body and spirit, to meet their higher self. I use old Tibetan bowls, quartz crystal bowls, gongs, chimes, drums, voice, percussion and other original music to create a "bath of sound" to allow body, mind and spirit to create the harmonics you need. My work and the work of many other sound practitioners is available live and on recordings.

How can sound be part of your self-care? Likely you're already using sound in one way, by playing music you love. You have music to pick yourself up and music to calm down. Hopefully, there's music to fall asleep to and music to keep you alert while driving. Allow me to offer one suggestion, play it out loud. We live in a world of ear buds and noise canceling headphones and those are convenient and essential inventions. But your body benefits from sound, not only through your ears. It seeks to soak the vibration up through skin, bones, all of your nervous system. So sometimes, crank up the speakers and set those vibes free.

What other tools can bring sound into your self-care tool kits? Chimes (yes, those wind chimes hanging out on the porch), bells and drums. Oh yes! Drumming is fun for everyone, from your children to grandpa. We all have an innate sense of rhythm. Yours might feel a bit rusty from not using it, but drumming is a very effective vibration that body, mind, and spirit loves. Get a drum or tap on your desk or your breast bone. Have fun with it. Often there are community drum circles where you can explore rhythm. Those folks will welcome you with open arms whether or not you think you're any good. There is no such thing as wrong notes when we're using sound and vibration for healing. Set yourself free.

this journey

I mentioned shamans and journeying earlier. Let's elaborate a bit on that. Shamans use many methods to help themselves and their patients to shift their consciousness. The shaman can journey out into another plane of existence, seeking the solution to his/her patient's problem. The shaman can also send the patient off on a journey within to see more clearly what lesson their malady might teach them and how to resolve it. Shamans use different tools to help shift consciousness- chanting, plant medicine, but most commonly rattles and drums.

Drumming is a tool of entrainment. The healer plays the drum at a rhythm of the desired brain wave pattern. Our brains have a vibe too, of course. There are levels of brain wave frequency that relate to different physical, mental and emotional states.

Frequency band	Frequency	Brain states
Beta	12–35 Hz	Anxiety, active, external attention, relaxed
Alpha	8–12 Hz	Very relaxed, passive attention
Theta	4–8 Hz	Deeply relaxed, inward focused, meditation
Delta	0.5–4 Hz	Sleep

There are also gamma brain waves, which are a higher frequency, 35 Hz and higher. Gamma waves show a high level of focus, as the brain is very actively engaged, often problem solving.

The shamans most often worked with theta brain wave levels, playing their drums at around 220-240 beats per minute, targeting the low end of theta brain wave level. The magic happens regardless of what the person seeking help might be thinking about. The entrainment to the lower brain wave level occurs unconsciously. Of course, the voyage within can occur more easily when our intention is to move into the theta brain wave state. The shaman's rhythm helps seekers move into altered states and when the drumming stops, the seeker and the shaman are back to normal.

How can using healing sound in self-care help you?

Sound is an easy and very pleasant self-care tool- whether you are creating the sounds yourself or just playing a favorite tune. A key to the experience is to really listen. We often have music playing in the background of our lives, but in sound self-care, you want to focus more on the sound. Make sound the focal point of your quiet or meditative time.

How can using healing sound in self-care help the world?

Sound is often called a universal language, as it can draw people together so easily. Explore sounds, music and rhythms of the world. Attend music / drumming events to widen your community of sound lovers. Share your own music with love and compassion.

More sound online at SuniMoon.net

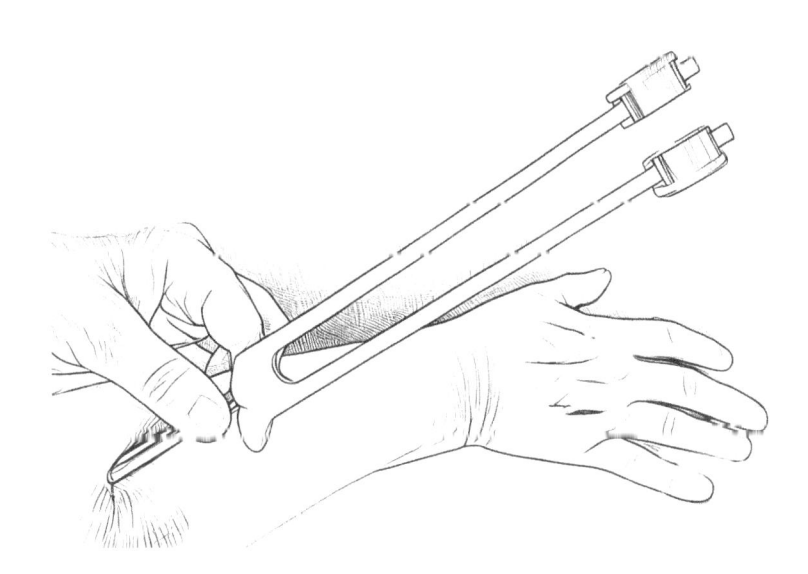

this journey

34

Stones- healers in the earth

Crystals and healing stones have been with us since the beginning of time. Their existence likely preceded plants, animals, and other sentient beings on the planet. Stones were created as our world was formed and continue to be forged as our planet changes. You could say that crystals and healing stones are part of the blueprint for planet Earth. This fact makes them really quite important; original equipment, if you will. All parts of our earth- each element, being, or entity has a unique and powerful purpose. You have a unique purpose. These stones have powerful purposes and maybe together you'll make some magic. My goal is to help you understand more about crystals, minerals and stones- how and why you might choose to use them in your life.

Most of what we call crystals and healing stones are minerals in different forms. Some stones are formed from just one mineral, while others are combinations of minerals. Certain minerals form beautiful crystals. Crystals of certain color, clarity and hardness are considered gem stones. Gems, like diamonds, emeralds, rubies, and others, might appear to be an ordinary rock in their natural state. Once cut and polished, their value is recognized in fine jewelry. Other minerals combine to grow into an amazing array of beautiful colors, texture, weight, resonance, and energies.

What is a crystal?

We might think of a crystal as a beautiful object with flat, regular geometric faces. To a gemologist, the definition of a crystal isn't about the visual but is about atoms. A crystal is a solid, with atoms arranged in a crystal system. There are seven types of crystal systems, each one resulting in a different physical

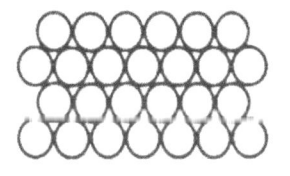

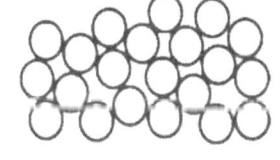

Crystalline   Amorphous

geometry, but they all share atoms which are arranged in tightly ordered, repeating lattice-like patterns. Any mineral whose atoms are arranged in one of these patterns is a crystal or designated as crystalline. When struck, these crystalline lattices will split along clean, smooth surfaces, which is how gemstones are faceted.

Crystals and healing stones exist all over the world. They can form when molten material cools or when elements precipitate out of liquid because of changes in concentrations, temperatures and pressure. While some crystals and stones form only in specific areas of the world, other stones are found all over the world. Crystals have fascinating differences in color and structure, depending on conditions under which they were formed- what elements were present, what temperature and pressure.

Natural geologic processes on the earth form most crystals and healing stones inorganically. Others can form organically within living creatures. An example is a weddelite crystal, which forms at the bottom of the Weddel Sea in Antarctica but is also found in human kidney stones. The human body contains many crystalline components. Calcium phosphate crystals make up the skeleton. We keep our balance because of calcite crystals in the inner ear. Apatite micro crystals form our tooth enamel. Some feel that our attraction to crystals and the basis for some of the healing work done with crystals is because crystals are a natural part of our bodies.

You may think of crystals as rarities, but in truth, most of the stones that make up our earth are crystalline. Quartz crystals are a commonly known crystal. Quartz makes up about 12 percent of the land surface and about 20 percent of the Earth's crust.

Historic and ritual use

The history of crystals and healing stones is a very long, winding road. The most valuable members of the mineral kingdom today are the precious gems used in our finest jewelry. However, there was a time in history when the value of gems was based less on market price and more on perceived healing powers. In the earliest days of humanity, we have signs of the use of these gems as amulets and talismans. The ancient people in Great Britain used Baltic amber, dated to 30,000 years ago, to create protectve charms. We have written reference to crystals from ancient Sumeria from 800-900 BCE.

Ancient Egyptians used stones such as clear quartz, lapis lazuli, carnelian, turquoise, and emeralds in amulets and jewelry to help ensure health and safety. They used chrysolite to drive out evil spirits and soothe the sufferers of night terrors. Amethyst, carnelian, emerald and lapis lazuli was commonly used in their tombs, placed on the body or carved into sarcophagi over the third eye to help guide the deceased to the afterlife.

The word "crystal" originates from "ice" in ancient Greek. The Greeks believed that clear quartz was water frozen so deeply it would be solid forever. "Amethyst" is also from the ancient Greek language, meaning "not drunken." People used this stone then, as they do today, to help support avoidance of alcohol and its side effects.

Theophrastus, a student of Aristotle, is believed to have written the first book about stones and crystals. The book *Peri Lithon* ('Of Stones') served as a reference of the healing power of gems, written around 315 BCE. In 77 CE, Pliny the Elder wrote *Historia Naturalus,* a part discussed precious stones and served as a resource until medieval times. The Greeks recommended rubbing magnetic lodestone on the skin to draw out pain and impurities. This is likely the first mention of using magnets in healing.

In early Japanese culture, quartz crystal spheres were used to foresee the future, as they are today. The Japanese revered quartz as their legend taught it was formed from the breath of a white dragon and was a symbol of perfection. Quartz crystal was important to seers and shamans in many cultures. The Australian Aboriginal myths refer to quartz crystal as *maban*, the source of a shaman's power. While highly valued in many areas of the world, jade was held in highest honor in ancient China. It was first prized for color and durability, being used in tools. Historians have dated jade carvings as early as the Neolithic period (3500-2000 BCE.) People believed jade would bring serenity, peace of mind and used it to protect infants.

Ayurveda, a natural method of healing originated in India over 8000 years ago, used gem tinctures made by soaking gemstones for varying periods of time. Hard gems, like diamonds or sapphires, were soaked for a month. Softer stones like pearls or coral were soaked for less time. Ashes of burned stones and gems were also used in making tinctures. Please note that not all stones or gems can survive soaking, nor are many crystals and stones safe for ingestion.

Monumental stones also play a role in healing and mysticism. Ancient civilizations all over the world placed stones in a circle. A well-known example is Stonehenge in Wiltshire, England, thought to have been constructed between 3000 to 2000 BCE. There is no clear record left from the peoples of these times, but archaeological evidence suggests it might have been a place of healing, burial, ceremony or astronomy. Some native people in North America use a medicine wheel, sometimes built of stones. The medicine wheel is a sort of map of a life and used to maintain health and get healing. These ancient structures or traditions have varied meanings and perceived uses. All involve a precise arrangement of stones geometrically or aligned to the sun or other planets. All interesting ways in which stones have been valued and empowered through the ages.

In ancient times, there was no separation between magic and medicine. Even the Christian church honored the healing powers of stones. In more modern times, writings about crystals and stones changed. In the early 1900s, books about gems and precious stones took one of two paths. They were factual accounts of the stone's physical characteristics or they described more mystical powers.

The New Age in the west (1970s) brought a powerful, renewed interest in the healing powers of stones. Along with this came growing knowledge of the energy healing practices and traditional medicine from the east. Gem and mineral shows, once solely for geology enthusiasts, became filled with people seeking rocks and minerals for their healing powers. Contemporary books, documenting these energetic and healing powers of crystals and stones were in demand. Healers using these ancient tools were more accepted and sought after.

We live in a time where the divisions between traditional medicine and these alternatives are beginning to blur. It is common to talk to people who use both forms of healing, the alternative therapies providing support to mainstream treatments.

From ancient times, disease (dis-ease) has been perceived as an outward manifestation of an imbalance in the body, mind or spirit. Traditional Chinese medicine, Ayurvedic medicine and other shamanic practices work to sense and correct imbalances before disease shows up in the physical body. Modern medicine is called in to action once diseases are expressed in the body, but often, their focus is to mitigate symptoms. There is a growing interest in modern medicine to look at these more ancient practices. Crystals are just one alternative healing technique that you can use to keep your body well and in balance or as a supplement to modern medicine's solutions.

Crystals can help balance brain waves. Our thoughts have a direct effect on our bodies. Living in fear of disease or assuming that disease will come can create a physical environment where disease is more likely to manifest. Crystals aren't some magic wand, but they can focus energy where desired. That can mean that you might use the energy to calm a worried mind in order that your higher, wiser self might be free to direct your thoughts in a more productive, healing manner.

In healing, it is so important to consider that your body's natural state is health. Your body wants to stay healthy and in balance. Sometimes stress, diet, lack of exercise and many other things can throw your body out of balance. Crystals and healing stones can be one way to add supportive energy to your body's energy system, helping it to better accomplish its healing goals. It isn't necessary to become deeply educated when you consider working with crystals to heal. Hold a crystal in your hands and try to visualize/ imagine healing energy flowing through your body, head to toe. Imagine your body's energy system being lit up with a bright light that the crystals can magnify and direct for you. Directing the crystal's energy isn't necessary and often not even wise. Rather, allow the crystal energy to flow through your body, clearing blockages that might exist and sustaining perfect balance in body, mind and spirit. Working in this way reinforces that healing and health are our normal states.

To choose a stone, learn how to use and care for them, I suggest you check out your local rock shop or metaphysical store. There you'll find books, stones and kindred spirits to help you along your path. The stones are the oldest people, therefore the wisest. They have endured so much. Allow them to help you connect the physical and the spiritual, the visible and the invisible, the practical/logical with the magical. Have fun.

How can working with stones and crystals help you?

Stones and crystals are beautiful. Of course, I've always been that person who never comes home from a hike without a stone in my pocket. I like to think that nature is a wonderful healer, so if stones and crystals resonate with you, why not invite them into your world? Right now, even though I'm writing from the road, there are 2 stones sitting right by my computer. They feel like friends, a calming force and help, however I might need it. Perhaps they can also help you.

How can working with stones and crystals help the world?

I like to think that natural solutions are good. However, as with many things in our world today, we must be conscious of how many stones are mined, how they are taken and whether they are in their natural state or have been electrically or chemically treated. Be sensitive to how the stones are removed from Mother Earth. Find a rock and gem shop near you and go there. Talk to them about where their products come from. I have found people at rock shops LOVE to talk about rocks and are amazing resources of information. Bear in mind, too, that a healing stone might be one you dug out of your garden. Not all important stones look like clear crystals. Trust how the rock came to you and how it feels to you. Sense its message and purpose. Sometimes, the rocks tell me, "take me home." And then I do.

35

Connection and community

You've taken quite a journey with me. I'm so very grateful. I have been called to this work of teaching, sharing, healing and awakening since I was a little girl. But honestly, I've not shared my mission much with others. In recent years, I worked in healing and sound, but would have felt presumptuous in talking about enlightenment. Now, the world has changed and my mission is clearer. I'm called to talk more openly about what I do to whoever might cross my path.

I may never know you or how you crossed my path. But allow me to give you this one last bit of help… talk to others. I'm not suggesting you stand on the corner and preach. I'm also Really Not suggesting you tell people, "You know what you need to do." I hope you might find kindred spirits where you can share your purpose, your questions, what hopes burn brightly in you. Finding community empowers us. My family doesn't understand energy, light, healing, meditation, sound as I do, but they value me. My chosen community is the place where I feel seen and that place is where I can grow. I encourage you to find a place in the circle, a seat at the table where you are welcome, supported and valued. That is so important to each of us.

How to find community? This is such a valid question. If you live in a small town that honors old ways and traditions, it might be hard to find a community that fits your needs and purpose. Some people have better results from creating community through holding workshops or events. Drum circles, or meditation gatherings can be a place to start. Some people have used the MeetUp app to find kindred spirits. Is there a rock shop or metaphysical store near you? Go there and meet those fine folks. Sometimes, you might have to go to a larger city near you to find community. Social media can also provide some powerful connections for all of us.

this journey

At this point, I imagine building some sort of online community. All I can do now is direct you to ThisJourney.us my resource site. As time goes on, I visualize we can build a community there. Until then, we all need our light community, our energy community, our love community. I'm hoping you will imagine, visualize, dream yours into existence.

There are enlightened communities all over this planet doing amazing, loving and compassionate work. Never ever feel that you're alone or a bit too weird, as I often have. You were made for these times. You were made to fulfill your purpose, as you have so far in life, and will continue to as we all grow into our brighter, more loving and compassionate future.

Gathering as a community will help you… your community will help the world.

On closing

This final chapter is my time to encourage you. I hope you find a few practices in this book that resonate with you. Do them, change them, learn more about them, allow them to expand your horizons. Consider your daily practice. Can you add thoughts, actions, or rituals that will encourage you every day? Consider eliminating those activities that don't lift you up. Create an alternate routine to use when worry or anxiety sets in.

This process of connecting your physical self with your spiritual self is the gist of awakening. This enlightenment brings with it a sense that you have nothing to fear in this life. You are here to help. You have all the strength, wisdom, and energy to be all you are meant to be. No hoops to jump through. No certifications needed. You are ready, and now is your time.

Awakening is an accessible state. You have enlightenment in you, but you must open to it. Add daily practices to your life to deepen your neural pathways to your higher self. Care for and allow yourself to embrace this higher, wiser, loving, compassionate being you are meant to be in this world. Some days the connection will feel strong, other days the dog will pee in your shoe, you will be impatient with a friend, you'll wonder if there's any hope for us. Then breathe deep and reconnect- enlightenment.

To be alive at this time of previously unknown transformation is a true privilege. There were many souls who wished to come here, who wanted to be here in a body and they could not. You are here. Your purpose is mighty. Open your heart and mind, allow the gratitude and love to flow in and through you.

Your purpose will likely never make headlines or bring you fame. That sort of power isn't what the world needs. It needs your special, unique wonder. Your purpose may help a few, then they may help a few more, and so on. This global awakening will take time, but you are integral to empowering this transformation to happen more quickly, more completely, and with more love and compassion.

Find a few folks, a bit of community, a tiny tribe, and share what you've learned. I'm not suggesting you tell them about me or these practices. It's more important that you share about your purpose. When I started trying to explain my purpose to others, I was sure no one would understand. But a few did. And they offered me suggestions, ideas to help me do my work more fully, and ways to share the concepts more smoothly. One thought was that I should write a book about simple enlightenment. Who knew?

Thank you for all you do. Thank you for your light. Please don't doubt yourself and your power. Never be afraid to shine your light. You aren't called to sell anything, or preach from the street corner- you are called to be more truly you. Your job is to be more loving, be more compassionate. Connect with the power of your body, mind, emotions and spirit- all working together. You too will help me and millions of others to bring light, love and peace to our world.

The light, love and wisdom in me sees the very same and more in you. May we always walk through this life in ways that might encourage others to see their own light, love, and wisdom.

Suni

Suni Moon is a creative, transformative teacher- sharing ancient practices in new ways to calm and awaken body, mind and spirit. Visit her website at SuniMoon.net for access to more of her work and services. Her resource site is ThisJourney.us
Suni's healing, meditative music is playing on streaming services and is available for purchase.

Visit SuniMoon.net/readers for links to recordings of meditations from this book and more.

More from the author

Suni Moon is a sound healer working in Milwaukee Wisconsin in the US. She is a sound artist and energy healer creating environments that are conducive to calming, healing and awakening to your higher purpose. She plays for individual clients in person at her studio. Her healing music is also available through BandCamp or you can find her on popular streaming services.

Her intuitive skills allow her to work remotely with clients all over the world. She offers Your SoulSong, a 10-12 minute sound healing meditation that she composes and records just for you. More info and music at YourSoulSong.net

This is her first book. Other offerings include video and audio classes and experiences available on her resource site. You'll find live events there also. Visit ThisJourney.us

References

1- Definitions are sourced from Oxford Languages dictionary- https://languages.oup.com/google-dictionary-en/

2- Thich Nhat Hahn- "Zen Master Thich Nhat Hanh is a global spiritual leader, poet and peace activist, revered around the world for his pioneering teachings on mindfulness, global ethics and peace." https://plumvillage.org/about/thich-nhat-hanh, pg. 11, 98

3- Daniel Quinn- "author of Ishmael, the novel that in 1991 won the Turner Tomorrow Fellowship, established to encourage authors to seek "creative and positive solutions to global problems."- https://www.ishmael.org pg. 17, 20

4- Info on hunger in the US- Share Our Strength, 1030 15th Street, NW, Suite 1100 W, Washington DC, 20005 http://www.nokidhungry.org pg. 18

5- How close is the Amazon tipping point? Forest loss in the east changes the equation, Liz Kimbrough, 20 SEP 2022, Monga Bay- telling impactful stories of biodiversity loss, climate change, https://news.mongabay.com/2022/09/how-close-is-the-amazon-tipping-point-forest-loss-in-the-east-changes-the-equation/ pg. 19

6- News consumption FCC- key cross-cutting issues, Section 4, News Comsumption, pg. 20- https://transition.fcc.gov/osp/inc-report/INoC-20-News-Consumption.pdf   pg. 25

7- Gorillas in our midst: sustained inattentional blindness for dynamic events, D Simons, C F Chabris, PMID: 10694957 DOI: 10.1068/p281059- http://www.chabris.com/Simons1999.pdf pg. 25

8- Bill Plotkin, Nature & the Human Soul: Cultivating Wholeness & Community in a Fragmented World, Animas Valley Institute | Nature-Based Soul Initiation, https://www.animas.org pg. 30

9- Robert A Johnson- an American Jungian analyst and author with book sales over 3 million copies. pg. 31

10- Ram Dass- a prominent Harvard psychologist, psychedelic pioneer and teacher of spiritual practices- https://www.ramdass.org/being-love/ pg. 31

11- Paul Selig- educator, writer and spiritual channel-https://paulselig.com pg. 36, 47

12- Mary Oliver- an award winning American poet- MaryOliver.com pg. 40

13- Lee Harris- energy intuitive, channeler, author, and musician http://www.LeeHarrisEnergy.com pg. 51

14- Malcolm Gladwell- a Canadian journalist, author, and public speaker.https://www.gladwellbooks.com pg. 54

15- Robert Frost- American poet, 1874-1063, pg. 59

16- Sam Harris "Waking Up: A Guide to Spirituality Without Religion- https://www.samharris.org pg. 62

17- Matthieu Ricard- monk, humanitarian, author, photographer- matthieuricard.org pg. 72

18- Research with thought-sampling techniques has shown that an average of 47 percent of our time is spent with our mind wandering.- https://www.psychologytoday.com/us/blog/facilitating-thought-progression/202402/let-your-mind-wander pg. 72

19- Understanding the subconscious Mind- Mike Kitko- coach, speaker, author- https://www.linkedin.com/pulse/understanding-subconscious-mind-mike-kitko/ pg. 77

20- Albert Einstein quote- sourced https://www.goodreads.com/quotes/143906-as-our-circle-of-knowledge-expands-so-does-the-circumference pg. 86

21- An interfaith exploration of light representation in the celebration, practice and interpretation of religion. https://blog.hartfordinternational.edu/2021/07/02/interfaith-representation-of-light-in-religion/ "From an article July 2nd, 2021 | Hartford International University pg. 86

22- Dr. Fritz Albert Popp- world-famous biophysicist and insightful researcher https://prlabs.com/blog/biophoton-fritz-albert-popp.html pg. 88

23- Plato quote- from 2.7: The Republic By Plato (Translated by Benjamin Jowett), https://human.libretexts.org/Courses/Los_Medanos_College/Classical_Greek%3A_Philosophy_Reader_(Haven)/02%3A_Chapters/2.07%3A_The_Republic_By_Plato_(Translated_by_Benjamin_Jowett)   pg. 92

24- Dr. Wayne Dyer- Internationally renowned author and speaker in the fields of self-development and spiritual growth- https://www.drwaynedyer.com   pg. 105

25- Forming habits- https://www.scientificamerican.com/article/how-long-does-it-really-take-to-form-a-habit/15- foot note about world health organization talking about alcohol states - self care is world care   pg. 108

26- Andy Caponigro author of The Miracle of the Breath: Mastering Fear, Healing Illness, and Experiencing the Divine, January 20, 2005   pg. 119

27- "Talk to yourself like someone you love."–Brené Brown, from her book, ""Talk to yourself like someone you love" appears in Brené Brown's book Daring Greatly: How the Courage to Be Vulnerable Transforms the Way We Live, Love, Parent, and Lead"   pg. 126

28- Mahatma Gandhi quote- ref https://www.goodreads.com/quotes/760902-we-but-mirror-the-world-all-the-tendencies-present-in   pg. 127

29- Jerome Braggs- a highly-gifted Intuitive Guide, Channel, Energy Healer, Inspirational Speaker, Singer + Poet, and Soul Teacher.- https://jeromebraggs.com   pg. 129, 135

30- Hippocrates quote (Logan A. C., Selhub E. M. (2012). Vis Medicatrix naturae: Does nature "minister to the mind"? BioPsychoSocial Medicine, 6, 11. https://doi-org/10.1186/1751-0759-6-11). pg.133

31- World Economics Forum- How self-care leads to healthier communities and a healthier planet- https://www.weforum.org/stories/2022/07/self-care-healthier-communities/   pg. 140

32- World Health Organization, Alcohol Use, 08/21/2024- https://www.who.int/europe/news-room/fact-sheets/item/alcohol-use pg. 140

33- Richard Louv- author of the international bestseller last child in the woods: saving our children from nature-deficit disorder https://e360.yale.edu/features/ecopsychology-how-immersion-in-nature-benefits-your-health - https://richardlouv.com pg.160

34- Sandra Ingerman- a world-renowned practitioner of shamanic healing. She is also the author of "Awakening to the Spirit World", https://www.sandraingerman.com   pg. 115, 164

35- Robin Wall Kimmerer- " a mother, scientist, decorated professor, and enrolled member of the Citizen Potawatomi Nation." Author of "Braiding Sweetgrass"- https://www.robinwallkimmerer.com/ pg. 165

Index

A

Jeanne Achterberg 134
adolescent mentality 140
affirmations 104
Amazon rainforest 19
Andy Caponigro 119
anxiety 73
Aristotle 61, 179
atheist 9
aura 87
Automatic writing 153–155
autonomic nervous system 172
awakening 29, 185
Ayurveda 179

B

biography 57
biophoton 88
body awareness 81
body spirit balance 36, 39
body- natural healer 133
Jerome Braggs 129
brain wave 174, 181
breath 117
    Conscious breathing 119
    Deep breathing 118
breathing practice 73, 120
breathwork 122
Brené Brown 126
André Breton 154

C

ceremony 163–165, 167, 169
Change 20
change. 45
changed world 13
Channeling 153, 155, 157
Chinese proverb 37
Christopher Chabris 25
Clinton Ober 160
community 36, 40, 183
community, 186
connection 183
Consciousness 77
    higher mind 79
    subconscious 78
crystal 179
Crystals 177, 180–181

D

disease 180
divination tools 154
Sir Arthur Conan Doyle 154
Dr. Wayne Dyer 105
Drumming 174

E

Eastern medicine 134
education 44
Egyptians 179
elevate 48
emotional maturity 29
empower 47
energy 91, 94
    energy field 92
    energy healing 97

enlightenment 8
entrainment 172, 174
evangelize 47
evolve 20
excess wealth 18

F

fear 43
feeling prepared 113
fight-or-flight 117–118
forest bathing 159, 161
frequencies 171
Robert Frost 59

G

Mahatma Gandhi 127
god 23
Gorillas in our midst: sustained inattentional blindness for dynamic events 25
Warren Grossman 160
Guided meditations 151

H

Thich Nhat Hanh 98
harmonics 171–172
Sam Harris 62
healing 97, 133, 181
healing stones 177, 180
healing work 136
heart center 41
    head to heart 41
heart center. 125
higher self 48
higher wisdom 111
Hippocrates 133

I

imagine 133
inattention 25
infallible 110
Sandra Ingerman 164
inner wisdom 109, 111, 113
Intention 103, 105, 165
intention writing 106
interbeing 97–98

J

jade 179
Japanese culture 179
Robert Johnson 30
journaling prompts 62, 69

K

Kabir 119
Robin Wall Kimmerer 165

L

labels 61–62, 129
Lao Tzu 61
light 85
    Light in metaphysics 86
    Light in religion 86
    Light of science 85
Richard Louv 160
Love 32, 40, 46

M

magnetic healing 97
manifestation 103
Mantra 151
meditation 71, 143, 149

Take a deep breath 20
Meditation practices 71, 82, 141
    breathwork 98
mindfulness 72
Mindfulness practices 145, 151
Modern Medicine 134
Monumental stones 180
Suni Moon 186
Morning wake up 141
mother earth 161

N

natural healer 133
natural state 181
nature 159–161
Nature & the Human Soul: Cultivating Wholeness & Community 30
Nature Deficit Disorder 160
negative bias 143
negativity bias 64
nervous system 117
    Parasympathetic nervous system 117
    Sympathetic nervous system 117
new world 13, 18, 23, 25, 35
new world, 35
news media 35, 43

O

observer of your mind 71, 74
old world 13, 17, 24, 44
Mary Oliver 40

P

Paramahansa Yogananda 143
passions 68, 114

childhood 67
paying attention 35
perceptive blindness 25
physical 39
Pliny the Elder 179
Bill Plotkin, 30
Dr. Fritz-Albert Popp 88
purpose 40, 53, 69, 114, 185

Q

Quartz crystal 178–179
Daniel Quinn 17, 20
    Ishmael 17

R

Ram Dass 31
Matthieu Ricard 72
ritual 163–165, 167, 169

S

Sanskrit 31
self-care 130, 139, 173
self-deprecating comments 124
self-love 129
self-talk 126
Paul Selig 36, 47
separation 23
service 30
seven aspects of self-care 139
Shaman 134
Shamanism 134
shamans 174
share 47
sick care 139
Daniel Simons 25

Simple enlightenment 36
Sound 171, 173
    sound healing 171, 173, 175
sound healing 172
Speaking kindly 124
spirit 39
    higher self 42
Spiritualists 153
Stonehenge 180
study 52

T

taking action 51
The Fisher King and the Handless Maiden 30
Theophrastus 179
Thich Nhat Hanh 98
Transformation 164, 185
trauma healing 32, 63–64
tribal communities 18

V

visualization 103, 107
visualize 133
voice 123, 125

W

waveform 172
weddelite crystal 178
western medicine 134

Y

Paramahansa Yogananda 143
you are ready 51
your purpose 35